Extraordinary World

Robert Silverberg

Scientists and Scoundrels

A Book of Hoaxes

University of Nebraska Press
Lincoln and London

Manufactured in the United States of America

First Nebraska paperback printing: 2007

Library of Congress Cataloging-in-Publication Data

Silverberg, Robert.

Scientists and scoundrels: a book of hoaxes / Robert Silverberg.

p. cm.—(Extraordinary world)

Originally published: New York: Crowell, 1965.

Includes bibliographical references and index.

ISBN-13: 978-0-8032-5989-8 (pbk.: alk. paper)

ISBN-10: 0-8032-5989-1 (pbk.: alk. paper)

1. Science—Miscellanea. 2. Quacks and quackery. I. Title.

Q173.S59 2007

500—dc22

2006025435

Oh, what a tangled web we weave

When first we practice to deceive!

—Walter Scott: Marmion

Introduction

This is, in a way, a book of science fiction—or, at any rate, a book of fictional science. There are hardly any monsters from outer space in it, and only a single rocket ship. Our heroes and our villains are chiefly men of science, though. Sometimes even very learned men behave in strange and erratic ways, and their odd behavior forms the substance of the present book.

It is a book of hoaxes. It is a record of human attempts to bamboozle, flimflam, hoodwink, and otherwise deceive. The word "hoax" is not particularly old, as English words go; its first appearance in the language seems to have occurred only in 1796. Some say that it is derived from an older word, "to hocus," which dates from about 1640. A hocuser was one who deceived, juggled, stupefied, conjured. He was thought to use the Latin formula "hocus-pocus" in his trickery, Latin of course being the language of educated men who might be expected to befuddle ordinary mortals. The chapters to come will reveal the doings of a variety of hocusers and suspected hocusers.

The word may be fairly young, but hoaxing itself is an ancient art. The Bible provides us with several classic hoaxes, such as the one carried out by Jacob on his father Isaac. Isaac, growing old and blind, wished to bless his sons Esau and Jacob. Esau, as the first-born son, was entitled to the larger portion of his father's property. And, as Jacob observed, "Behold, Esau my brother is a hairy man, and I am a smooth man." Jacob donned the skins of goats, woolly side outward, and went before Isaac for the blessing. The old man put his hands on Jacob and felt the rough skin of the goats, and thought that he was blessing Esau, and so the wily Jacob stole his brother's blessing. Such was hoaxing in Biblical times.

Another foxy character of ancient days, Odysseus, was also fond of hoaxing. In the *Odyssey* we read how Odysseus and his men became prisoners in the cave of the one-eyed giant Polyphemus. The captives managed to blind the monster, but he guarded the mouth of the cave and they could not escape. Polyphemus did send his sheep and goats out of the cave to pasture, and ran his hands over the backs of the animals to see that no viii Greeks were riding out on them. But the Greeks had fastened themselves underneath the biggest animals, and slipped safely out under the giant's groping hands.

Odysseus had performed another act of flummery on the hapless Polyphemus. When he first arrived in the cave, Odysseus told the giant that his name was "No Man." Then, after the Greeks had blinded Polyphemus, the wounded giant roared in pain, and his friends called out, "Who has injured you?"

"No Man has injured me," Polyphemus answered— and so the neighboring giants did not come to his aid.

Hoaxes are entertaining things, at least for outsiders, though their victims rarely find them amusing. But why write a book about them? Is it useful or instructive in any way to read about frauds of science, to spend time learning of ersatz discoveries and mythical inventions?

I think it is. The study of hoaxes is not only a pleasant pastime, but a valuable form of education. As Little Buttercup sings in *H.M.S. Pinafore,* "Things are seldom what they seem." The task of science is to distinguish between the real and unreal, between fact and fantasy. The hoaxers, through their mischief, have done what they could to blur these distinctions. But the very fact that men do enjoy creating hoaxes teaches us all to be on our guard. We cannot accept statements at face value. We must check, and test, and examine, for things are seldom what they seem. Does a newspaper story say there are men on the moon? Yes, but is it so? Are there vast sea serpents? Perhaps, but let's look closely at the evidence. Was there a lost continent of Atlantis? Can a perpetual-motion machine be built? Perhaps. Perhaps. But first we must check.

The hoaxers teach us to check. They make us unsure of what we think we see—and that is useful. We have to challenge the evidence. If the tools of science are not good enough for telling fact from fantasy, we must develop new tools.

Here is a baker's dozen of hoaxes. If, reading about such characters as Mesmer and Koch and Keely, you feel a trifle uneasy about some of the things you see in the daily paper, so be it. Take a closer look at the latest wonders.

Things are seldom what they seem.

Contents

1: The Lying Stones
of Dr. Beringer

In the year 1710, some workmen digging near the city of Würzburg in southwestern Germany discovered what appeared to be an enormous bone, hard as rock and terribly heavy. There were those who said it must be the bone of a giant who had been drowned in Noah's Deluge—for, according to the Bible, "there were giants in those days."

Huffing and puffing, the workmen brought their find to the University of Würzburg, a venerable institution founded in 1403. The object was duly examined, and,

1

since it seemed to be a bone indeed, it was turned over to the faculty member who would know most about such things.

He was Dr. Johann Bartholomew Adam Beringer, Senior Professor and Dean of the Faculty of Medicine, Doctor of Philosophy and Medicine, and Chief Physician to the Prince-Bishop of Würzburg. Dr. Beringer, in short, was a very important man. He examined the bone with care. Before long, he pronounced his verdict.

It was not, he said, the bone of any giant man who had lived before the Deluge. (He was quite right: it was, as a matter of fact, the fossilized bone of a kind of elephant that had inhabited Germany some fifteen million years ago.) Dr. Beringer went on to add that it was not a bone at all, however much it might look like one. It was, he declared, pure stone—a *lusus naturae*, or "prank of nature."

Dr. Beringer was thereby stating one of the best-known theories of his day. For several centuries workmen had been digging up what seemed to be the relics of ancient animals and men. In the sixteenth and seventeenth centuries, many large buildings were constructed in Europe, requiring deep foundations, and the workers were finding curious things in the earth. Moreover, men were beginning to regard the world about them with great curiosity. They were stopping to examine things, instead of accepting everything in blind faith.

What were these strange relics? They were given the
2 name fossils, from the Latin word *fossilis*, meaning

"dug up." They seemed to be the bones of fish, or of giants, or of reptiles. There were even the fossil imprints of fragile plants and insects on rock. Some people— Leonardo da Vinci was one—said that these were, quite simply, the bones of dead creatures, buried in ancient floods and turned to stone over the ages. But that obvious explanation was too simple for many of the learned men. They had more elegant theories.

Some said that the fossils were not relics at all, but merely stones of unusual shape. Why, then, did they seem to look like bones or plants? Simply by the whim of God, the savants answered. The fossils were *lusi naturae*, pranks or sports of nature. What mere mortal could question the designs of God? If He chose to fashion stones so that they looked like the skeletons of fish, He must have had some far-reaching reason for doing so, and it was not ours to wonder why.

As for the actual means by which the fossils were formed, there were many suggestions. Some simply said that God had created them when He brought living plants and animals into being. Others suggested that under certain circumstances the seeds of plants or the eggs of fish might slip into cracks in the earth and "hatch" in the darkness to create fossil forms. Others talked of a life-giving mist from the sea, or of "fatty matter set into fermentation by heat," or of "a tumultuous movement of terrestrial exhalations," or of a "lapidific juice" that hardened to take the shape of fossils.

Dr. Beringer was of the school of thinking that felt   3

that fossils were simply "stones of a peculiar sort, hidden by the Author of Nature for His own pleasure." Since he held an important position at an important university, his views were widely quoted and accepted. Year after year, Beringer lectured his students on the nature of fossils. The good doctor, who was born in 1667, was himself the son of a famous professor, and his own reputation for scholarship and industriousness was of the highest.

But there were those who disagreed with Beringer's ideas. What's more, they disliked him personally. They thought he was arrogant in his learning, too intolerant of other beliefs. They set out to have some fun with Beringer. They gave him a very unpleasant surprise—and made his name immortal.

Beringer, good scholar that he was, had an abiding interest in collecting and studying fossils. He hired young men to dig in the hills near Würzburg and search for the miraculous "stones of a peculiar sort" that he found so interesting.

The early results were poor. Beringer's district, the duchy of Franconia, was a lovely place, with a placid river winding through level fields ringed by handsome mountains. The land was ideal for vineyards and farms, but did not seem to produce fossils. The disappointed Beringer had to fill his shelves with specimens sent him by friends in other lands.

4   Then, in the spring of 1725, Beringer's workmen be-

gan to dig on the slopes of one mountain that had been examined before, without success—and they struck scientific treasure, in Beringer's words "one bountiful horn of plenty."

There were three workmen: Christian Zänger, who was seventeen, and two brothers, Niklaus and Valentin Hehn, who were eighteen and fourteen, respectively. Beginning on May 31, 1725, they made a series of remarkable finds.

They found stones bearing pictures in raised relief. First came a stone showing the sun and its rays; then came two depicting worms. And then the deluge. The three workmen brought stone after stone to the delighted Beringer, until he had several hundred of them. Beringer later described the range of objects depicted on the stones in these glowing terms:

"Here, representing all the kingdoms of Nature, but especially those of animals and plants, are small birds with wings either spread or folded, butterflies, pearls and small coins, beetles in flight and at rest, bees and wasps (some clinging to flowers, others in their nests), hornets, flies, tortoises from sea and stream, fishes of all sorts, worms, snakes, leeches from the sea and swamp, lice, oysters, marine crabs, frogs, toads, lizards, cankerworms, scorpions, spiders, crickets, ants, locusts, snails, shell-bearing fishes, and countless rare and exotic figures of insects obviously from other regions. Here are nautili, ammonites, starfish of very different and delightful species, shells, spiral snails, winding shells, scallops, and 5 other heretofore unknown species. Here were leaves, flowers, plants, and whole herbs, some with and some without roots and flowers. Here were clear depictions of the sun and the moon, of stars, and of comets with their fiery tails."

Most remarkable—"the supreme prodigy commanding the reverent admiration of myself and my fellow examiners"—Beringer beheld certain tablets inscribed in Latin, Arabic, and Hebrew characters. Some of the stones bore single letters, others whole words. Some letters were shaped well, others crudely. Occasionally an image of a scallop or a snail would bear lettering on its back. Beringer consulted linguists and rabbis, and all gave him the same opinion: that the words formed the name of God, Jehovah. It was as though the Creator had chosen to take credit for the miraculous stones of Würzburg by signing His name to His handiwork.

Beringer was overjoyed. From June to November, his workmen delved into the mountain, until, when winter forced a halt, there were two thousand figured stones in all. Beringer spent the winter months writing a book about the great discovery. He intended to tell the world that his theories of fossils had been triumphantly vindicated. Nobody could say that these stones were the bones of dead beasts drowned in the Deluge. No, they were works of art, the products of God, Beringer insisted. Nor was this man a fool; bear in mind that he was one of the preeminent scholars of his day.

6   While Beringer was at work on his book, certain dis-

turbing events occurred. Two of his colleagues at the university attacked the stones as frauds, and called Beringer an ignoramus. The stones, they said, had been "recently sculpted by hand, made to look as though at different periods they had been resurrected from a very old burial, and sold to Beringer as to one indifferent to fraud and caught up in the blind greed of curiosity." They went on to say that Beringer himself knew he had been fooled, and now was "deluding the world, and trying to sell new hoaxes as genuine antiques, to the silent laughter of prudent souls."

The names of these two attackers were J. Ignatz Roderick and Georg von Eckhart. Roderick was Professor of Geography, Algebra, and Analysis at the University of Würzburg; Eckhart, an older man, was the university's librarian, as well as Librarian to the Prince-Bishop of Würzburg.

They were not content simply to denounce Beringer. They manufactured a few figured stones themselves, and offered to sell them to him. Zänger, one of Beringer's diggers, brought him a few stones showing such things as a winged dragon, a mouse, and a lion. Beringer accepted them as genuine and paid Zänger for them. Then Roderick and Eckhart openly declared that they had carved those stones. They did not come right out and say they were responsible for the two thousand stones found earlier—but they left no doubt that those earlier finds were highly suspicious.

Another man might have hesitated and pondered a 7

bit. Not the dogmatic Dr. Beringer. He brushed aside the charges of Roderick and Eckhart as malicious gossip, and went on writing his book.

It was published in 1726 under the title, *Lithographiae Wirceburgensis*. Like most scholarly books of its day, it was in Latin. It bore elaborate dedications to Christopher Franz, Bishop of Würzburg and Duke of Franconia. A series of finely engraved plates showed the famous stones.

Beringer's book, which has recently been translated into English, makes lively and entertaining reading. His style was flowery and ornate, but he wrote clearly and vigorously. The extent of his learning is evident on every page. He had read nearly every word published on the subject of fossils, and was able to reply to the differing schools of thought with skill and power.

The stones, he made it clear at the outset, were not forgeries. "Many erudite scholars and illustrious men of letters," he said, "could not refrain from suspecting that some imposture lay hidden beneath these extraordinary mysteries—that the stones were fictitious and were fabricated in secret for purposes of fraudulent avarice." But this simply was not so, he said. The stones had been honestly found, hidden in the earth, treasures buried for centuries since God had shaped them.

He did admit that when one looked at the stones "one would swear that they are the work of a very meticulous sculptor." Many of them were soft, carved from some chalky material, with neatly outlined figures. The tiny

8

animals and insects displayed "splendid grace and elegance."

Beringer spoke of the *lusus naturae* theory. There were, he said, stones which "imitate the forms of other bodies," and which were the result of "Nature playing artistically." Many of the relics that men called the remains of ancient creatures actually were of this sort.

He was careful, though, to distinguish between his stones and fossils. Some fossils, Beringer conceded, really were animal remains. They had been left behind after some flood, perhaps, and had gradually turned to stone. But these, when broken open, displayed the internal structure of shell or bone. On the contrary, the stones he had found had "no joints or chambers" inside, "being an unformed stony mass." There was no possibility that the figures on his stones were the petrified remains of once-living creatures, he said. After all, many of the stones showed the complete bodies, not merely the bones, of such creatures as toads and frogs. Bees and wasps, crickets and beetles, all were represented down to the finest detail. These could be no petrified remains, for the fragile remains would long ago have decayed or been crushed. And what of the plants, flowers, and herbs, "by nature extremely frail," which "under heavy rain or frost, droop to the ground, drop their leaves, and die"? Could these have withstood the Deluge?

The stones bearing the name of God certainly were not fossils of anything. No, Beringer said, these were all the works of the Deity, in an artistic mood.

9

He rejected the idea that his stones were pagan idols, buried in the mountain by the Germans a thousand years before when they took up Christianity. Though it was customary, he said, for the pagans to fashion crude images of plants, trees, and animals, his stones were not of that sort. The pagans had worshipped "monsters and fierce beasts. But who can recall crickets, spiders, worms, tortoises, and similar castoffs of Nature being raised to an altar and endowed with divinity?"

Beringer brushed aside the ugly charge that the stones were recently carved. "Vicious raillery, false rumors and gossip," he declared. But he did see "unmistakable indications of the sculptor's knife" on his stones, while refusing to believe that that knife could have been wielded by anyone but God. He declared that "God, the Founder of Nature, would fill our minds with His praises and perfections radiating from these wondrous effects, so that, when forgetful men grow silent, these mute stones might speak with the eloquence of their figures."

In chapter after chapter, Beringer demolished all opposition to his stones. He proved, at least to his own satisfaction, that they were what he thought they were. His enemies, he said, had brought his "reputation to the brink of destruction" with their charges of fraud, but he did not doubt that he would prevail. Perhaps a few of the stones were counterfeits made by Roderick and Eckhart, he conceded, but the overwhelming majority of them were genuine beyond doubt. He closed his book by promising a further edition listing new discoveries in his "search for truth."

Beringer's book was published early in 1726. It was printed at great cost to its author, but was purchased enthusiastically by scholars who wished to read in detail of Beringer's wonderful discoveries. For a brief and dazzling moment, all Europe was agog with talk of Dr. Beringer and his miraculous figured stones.

Hardly was the book published, though, when a startling thing happened: Beringer tried to buy back the copies that had been sold, with the intention of destroying them! The famous stones, he admitted in grief, were the frauds that the skeptics said they were. He had been duped. He was a laughingstock. His handsome book, with its lovely plates, was a monument to his own blindness, and now he wanted only to burn every copy.

We do not know what made Beringer change his mind about the stones. One story has it that he dug up a stone that bore his own name—and suddenly saw that someone had been playing games with him. Or, possibly, he simply reconsidered the whole affair, and realized that the stones obviously were the work of pranksters out to mock him.

The exposure of the hoax made Beringer's book a collector's item. People who had bought it for study now kept it to chuckle over. Others sought to buy copies, and offered high prices. It was in such demand that in 1767 a German publisher brought out a second edition, purely 11 as an amusing curiosity. Beringer had been dead since 1740, so he did not have to witness this new display of his shame.

There was great scandal and outcry in Würzburg when the hoax was revealed. Beringer was a famous man of the town, and anything that brought disgrace on him hurt the reputation of all Würzburg. For if so important a scholar as Beringer could be gulled so easily, what did that say about the general level of intelligence in Würzburg?

An official inquiry was held to get to the bottom of the matter. In our day, when it was discovered that certain television quiz shows were being rigged, it was a congressional committee that investigated. The Beringer fiasco was the same sort of scandal in its time, and an inquiry was held starting on April 13, 1726. Beringer himself asked for it, for the "saving of his honor."

The first session took place at the Würzburg Cathedral. Many leading figures of the city were there to hear the dean of the church question the three young workmen who had found the stones.

The man on the spot was seventeen-year-old Christian Zänger, who had brought Beringer the stones that Roderick and Eckhart claimed they had fashioned. The other two workmen, the brothers Niklaus and Valentin Hehn, seemed innocent of all fraud. The Hehns declared under oath at the first session and again at the second, at the City Hall on April 15, 1726, that they had never ground or polished or sculpted any of the stones themselves, nor

12

planted them in the ground to be discovered later, nor done anything else shady or dishonest. "If we could make such stones," said Valentin Hehn, "we wouldn't be mere diggers."

Zänger, though, had a different tale to tell. He admitted receiving some stones from Roderick, "to which Roderick had applied a knife and carved the letters and the rest of the things." Roderick had given him a stone with a pomegranate on it, and one with a dragon, and one on which there was a lion with a long tail. He had delivered these to Beringer, who had paid him the usual fee. Roderick, too, had paid him. But he was vague about why Roderick wanted him to deliver false stones to Beringer.

A recess was called. Zänger was warned by the interrogators "to improve his memory of the actual events and truth." In the afternoon, he was questioned again. He admitted that Roderick had claimed to have buried some stones for the Hehns and Zänger to find. He also declared that Roderick had ordered him to try to trick Beringer into buying the false stones. Zänger had a complaint to make, too: he told the investigators that Roderick still owed him wages for eight days of stone-polishing, and could they help him collect?

Strangely, Roderick and Eckhart were never questioned—or, if they were, no record of the proceedings has survived. Soon after the incident, Roderick left Würzburg, obviously in disgrace. Eckhart seems to have kept his position as court librarian. Poor Beringer returned to his classrooms, a saddened and humiliated man. The story is often told that he "died of shame" as soon as the hoax was exposed, but in reality he lived fourteen more years, and published at least two other books. He never spoke of figured stones again. His reputation as a scholar was destroyed.

The lying stones of Dr. Beringer, it seems, were the work of Roderick, Eckhart, and Zänger, who must have spent many a long hour carving and polishing them and hauling them out to the mountain, planting them to be found later. It was no mere student prank, as is often claimed, but a deadly attack by two scholars on a third. Roderick and Eckhart may have feuded with Beringer in some way of which we have no knowledge. Zänger testified that they wanted to harm Beringer "because he was so arrogant and despised them all."

The Beringer hoax helped to seal the fate of the *lusus naturae* idea. Scholars less and less talked of fossils as "stones of a peculiar sort, hidden by the Author of Nature for His own pleasure." The Beringer stones had indeed been of a peculiar sort, but no one now could seriously think that the old ideas on how fossils were formed had any value. Gradually, men came to accept Leonardo da Vinci's suggestion that the fossils were the remains of creatures of a former age. The cruel trick played on Dr. Beringer helped to establish the modern theory of the antiquity of the world. The grotesque skeletons found in the earth could no longer be deemed sports of nature. Instead scientists realized that they

14

were probably relics of species long since extinct.

Poor Beringer! He paid a steep price for his gullibility. He remains famous today as the classic example of the scholar so wrapped up in his own theories that he failed to see beyond the end of his nose. Everyone could tell that the wonderful stones were frauds—everyone but Beringer, who spent a fortune publishing his book and a second fortune trying to buy the copies back.

The hoaxers, successful though they were, did not benefit from their exploit. They had hurt their own reputations as badly as they had hurt Beringer's, for he was popular in Würzburg and drew sympathy from everyone. Eckhart died four years after the scandal, in 1730. Roderick, who was then living in Cologne, wrote to the Prince-Bishop of Würzburg, asking to be allowed to return and put his dead friend's library in order. The Prince-Bishop answered in stiff terms, and was obviously not enthusiastic about having the hoaxer come back.

"In the past," he wrote to Roderick, "you have gained an unenviable reputation and have suffered no small blight on your good name." He trusted, therefore, "that henceforth you will acquit yourself more satisfactorily in your teaching of geography and algebra, and will so conduct yourself in all matters that whatever is deemed fitting may be more confidently entrusted to you."

Many of the wondrous stones still exist, and are on display in German museums. They are lovely to behold —and sad little reminders of a once-famed scholar remembered today only for his gullibility.

2: *The Marvelous Magnetism of Dr. Mesmer*

The year was 1778, and gay, glittering, sophisticated Paris had a new craze: animal magnetism. Some called it "mesmerism," after its inventor, the Austrian physician Franz Anton Mesmer.

Mesmerism was all the rage—especially among the wealthy women of the Parisian nobility. Mesmerism claimed to cure all ills; it left Dr. Mesmer's patients feeling tranquil and healthy and invigorated. It was unusual, it was exciting, and it was new. The ladies in their gaudy finery and the counts and barons in their powdered wigs flocked to the richly appointed house of Dr. Mesmer to take the treatment.

The house was magnificent. Mirrors covered the walls of its stately rooms, shimmering chandeliers shed a mystic light, the fragrance of incense and orange blossoms delighted the nostrils, and hidden harps tinkled softly. In the room where the treatment was administered there stood what Mesmer called the *baquet*—an oval tub, about a foot deep and four feet across. In the *baquet* were placed bottles of "magnetized water," corked tightly, their necks pointing outward. Water was poured in to cover the bottles, and iron filings sprinkled over them, for iron was known to be highly magnetic. The *baquet* was covered with an iron lid pierced with holes. Long movable rods of iron jutted through these holes.

The patients assembled themselves around the *baquet*. Dr. Mesmer instructed them to sit close together, pressing their knees against one another, and holding hands, so that the mysterious force called animal magnetism could flow through their bodies. Then they were to reach forward and grasp the iron rods projecting from the *baquet*. More magnetism would enter them. They were told to touch such parts of their bodies as might be diseased or afflicted against the rods.

Now strong, handsome young men entered the room. They were the "assistant magnetizers," from whose fingertips there flowed the mystic magnetic power. They began to stroke and massage the patients, looking them straight in the eyes. This was carried out in the greatest 17 silence, but gradually the sounds of a piano could be heard, and the voice of a concealed soprano, intoning a wordless melody.

Gradually the patients clustered round the *baquet* became strangely excited. The cheeks of the ladies began to glow; some started to scream, others to sob and tear their hair, or laugh till tears rolled down their cheeks. Now, wielding an imposing white "magnetic" wand, Dr. Mesmer himself took charge. A wave of the wand and the assistants scurried away. Garbed in a long robe of lilac-colored silk, richly embroidered with gold flowers, Mesmer came striding solemnly toward his patients. He silenced the screams and sobs with a single glance of his awe-inspiring eyes. With a stroke of his wand, with a gesture of his supple fingers, he made the patients grow calm. Some said they could feel streams of cold or burning vapor pass through their bodies as he gesticulated with fingers or wand. Eventually they were strangely relaxed, lost in a weird sleep. A snap of the finger, and the session ended. The patients, still a trifle dazed, paid their fees and filed out. They were not sure what had happened to them, but they knew it had been an exciting experience, good material for drawing-room conversation.

An eyewitness to one of Mesmer's sessions described the scene this way:

"The patients in their different conditions present a very varied picture. Some are calm, tranquil, and experience no effect. Others cough, spit, feel slight pains,

18

local or general heat, and have sweatings. Others again are agitated and tormented with convulsions. These convulsions are remarkable in regard to the number affected with them, to their duration and force. As soon as one begins to be convulsed, several others are affected. . . . These convulsions are characterized by the precipitous, involuntary motion of all the limbs, and of the whole body . . . by the dimness and wandering of the eyes, by piercing shrieks, tears, sobbing, and immoderate laughter. They are preceded or followed by a state of languor or reverie, a kind of depression, and sometimes drowsiness. The smallest sudden noise occasions a shuddering; and it was remarked, that the change of measure in the airs played on the piano-forte had a great influence on the patients. A quicker motion, a livelier melody, agitated them more, and renewed the vivacity of their convulsions.

"Nothing is more astonishing than the spectacle of these convulsions. One who has not seen them can form no idea of them. The spectator is as much astonished at the profound repose of one portion of the patients as at the agitation of the rest. . . . All are under the power of the magnetizer; it matters not in what state of drowsiness they may be, the sound of his voice—a look, a motion of his hand—brings them out of it."

Mesmer was a charlatan who grew rich from the foolishness of his patients, but the strange part of his story is that his notion of animal magnetism is still with us today, and is widely used in medicine as well as in the 19 world of entertainment. We call it hypnotism. Mesmer was the world's first hypnotist, but he concealed the merits of his discovery under a cloak of mumbo jumbo and fraud, labeling the whole package "animal magnetism."

The force known as magnetism has long fascinated men, and for good reason. It seems almost magical, almost supernatural, to see iron drawn toward a magnet. The ancient Greeks knew the mineral called lodestone, an oxide of iron which had the ability to attract iron, and called it Magnet, since it was found in the territory of Magnesia, in Thessaly. A thousand years ago, the Chinese were making use of the earth's magnetic field to build the direction-finding instruments we call compasses; during the Crusades, the compass found its way to Europe.

No one knew why magnets worked, and that added to their mystery. (Even today, though there is much talk of spinning electrons and magnetic molecules, a great many of the whys of magnetism remain unexplained.) Not very surprisingly, during the Middle Ages men began to credit magnets with mystic and occult powers.

Paracelsus, the great alchemist of the sixteenth century, was the first of the magnetizers. Paracelsus—he was a Swiss whose real name was Theophrastus Bombastus von Hohenheim—was a doctor as well as an alchemist, and he taught that the magnet could cure all diseases. One of his most popular medicines was a magnetic stone he called *azoth,* which he said cured epilepsy, hysteria, and other ailments. His fame spread throughout Europe; a whole school of magnetic doctors sprang up.

They were quacks, of course, but their mystical magnetic marvels sometimes got results. It is well known that a great deal of disease is "all in the mind"—psychosomatic disease, it is called. Very often, these imaginary ailments responded splendidly to magnetic treatment. A patient who had faith in magnetism could unconvince himself that he was sick just as easily as he had originally convinced himself.

An important magnetist of the seventeenth century was Sebastian Wirdig, Professor of Medicine at the University of Rostock in Germany. In 1673 he published a book called *The New Medicine of the Spirits,* in which he said that all living things gave off magnetic forces. A Spaniard named Balthazar Gracian declared that "The magnet attracts iron; iron is found everywhere; everything, therefore, is under the influence of magnetism." Magnetism, he said, caused all human emotion and thought as well as disease.

About a century later, a Jesuit priest with the curious name of Maximilian Hell carried out some research into the medical uses of magnetism. Father Hell, Professor of Astronomy at the University of Vienna, experimented in 1771 and 1772 with a healing method that involved applying odd steel plates to the body. In 1774, he com-   21 municated his ideas to Franz Anton Mesmer—and soon wonders were spawned.

Mesmer, born in Austria in 1734, had studied theology and medicine in Germany and at Vienna. When Father Hell told him about magnetism, Mesmer was a successful physician, and already familiar with the theories of Paracelsus. Mesmer believed that an invisible magnetic fluid filled the universe. He also claimed that he could control the flow of this fluid and use it to heal. He called the magnetic force of the human body *animal* magnetism to distinguish it from the more familiar magnetism of lodestone and iron bars.

He began to experiment with Father Hell's magnetic plates. Soon enough the two men quarreled. "Mesmer is a physician whom I have employed to work under me," Hell declared, probably correctly. Mesmer took offense, claimed that he and not the priest had invented the method, and accused Hell of trying to steal his ideas. In the resulting furor, Mesmer decided that it was best to leave Vienna, where Father Hell had many powerful friends. He moved his base of operations to Switzerland.

While treating one patient, Mesmer made an important discovery—the magnetic plates were unnecessary. The patient was one Miss Esterline, who suffered from dizziness, delirium, and rushes of blood to the head. Mesmer found that he could "cure" her simply by making slow passes through the air with his hands, which he said bathed her in the magnetic fluid emanating from his fingers.

22

He wrote to all the learned societies of Europe, telling of his magnetic theories and asking scientists to aid him in his research. Most ignored him; some simply called him a quack. Mesmer was undaunted. Magnetism, he said, was everywhere, and it was possible to magnetize not only such metals as iron, but everything. "I have rendered paper, bread, wool, silk, stones, leather, glass, wood, men, and dogs—in short, everything I touched—magnetic to a degree," he wrote a friend.

Mesmer experimented with magnetic cures in the hospitals of Berne and Zurich, and claimed to enjoy spectacular success. With these achievements behind him, he returned to Vienna hoping to confound his enemies. He took on the task of curing a Mademoiselle Paridis, who was blind and suffered from convulsions. Mesmer magnetized her several times.

"She is cured," he announced triumphantly.

Another physician examined her and reported that she was as blind as ever. Her family said that she still had convulsions. The facts did not agree with Mesmer's claims. "So much the worse for the facts," he seemed to say. "She is cured!"

This sort of claim did not impress the clear-eyed Viennese doctors. They suggested that Mesmer was practicing magic, and hinted that he would be wise to take his leave. Seeing a poor future for himself in Vienna, Mesmer left in 1778, and settled in Paris, a city of pleasure-loving people always willing to try the latest novelty.

Paris was made to order for Mesmer. He swiftly acquired an influential convert, a well-known doctor named D'Eslon, whose prestige helped win many patients. Parisian society swarmed to Mesmer's salon for treatments of animal magnetism. His methods grew ever more fanciful as his wealth increased; the magnetic devices became more elaborate, the solemn rigmarole of the sessions more theatrical. Going to Mesmer for treatment was almost like visiting the opera, one countess declared.

One of Mesmer's most loyal defenders was the Marquis de Lafayette, who had served with such valor during the recent revolution in America. When an academy to teach the new magnetic science was established, Lafayette invested the substantial sum of 100 gold louis. In 1784, Lafayette visited the United States, where he was a beloved figure, and carried the banner of mesmerism with him. With Mesmer's permission, Lafayette revealed some of the "secrets" of mesmerism to George Washington. In Philadelphia, Lafayette addressed the American Philosophical Society and enthusiastically told those learned gentlemen of Mesmer's wonderful work.

Meanwhile, in Paris, some of the more conservative doctors were troubled by Mesmer's success. "He has sold his soul to the devil," one doctor cried. Others called him a fraud, a charlatan, a dangerous madman.

Mesmer tried to get official government support. He wrote to Queen Marie Antoinette and asked for the gift of some large château where he could carry out his research in peace, untroubled by the cries of his enemies. He gently requested a small fortune to pay for his experiments. "In the eyes of your majesty," he declared, "four or five hundred thousand francs, applied to a good purpose, are of no account. The welfare and happiness of your people are everything. My discovery ought to be received and rewarded with a munificence worthy of the monarch to whom I shall attach myself."

The queen was not minded to oblige—but she did offer Mesmer twenty thousand francs, provided he had really made a genuine medical discovery and would allow his methods to be studied by a commission of doctors appointed by the government. Much as he coveted the money, Mesmer did not care to submit to official examination. He turned the offer down and left Paris for a five-month vacation.

The outcry against Mesmer grew noisier. While Mesmer was gone, his chief supporter, Dr. D'Eslon, took a bold step. He invited government inspection of *his* practice of animal magnetism. He said that he had nothing to hide, and that he welcomed a full investigation of mesmerism.

On March 12, 1784, the French king, Louis XVI, appointed four physicians to look into mesmerism. One of the four was Dr. Joseph Ignace Guillotin, whose invention, the guillotine, would lop off the monarch's head nine years later. The four doctors asked that five eminent men from other fields of endeavor be appointed to join the commission. One of the five was the great chemist Antoine Lavoisier, also destined to be a victim of the French Revolution. Another was Jean Bailly, an astronomer and historian. A third was Benjamin Franklin, the seventy-eight-year-old Philadelphia philosopher, then representing the infant United States in Paris.

Franklin immediately heard from his old friend Lafayette, who urged him to back Mesmer's claims. Franklin simply said he would consider the matter with an open mind, but was not optimistic. On March 19, he spoke of mesmerism as a "delusion," though he was willing to admit it might have some use. "There are in every great rich city," he wrote, "a number of persons who are never in health because they are fond of medicines and always taking them, whereby they derange the natural functions and hurt their constitutions. If these people can be persuaded to forbear their drugs in expectation of being cured by only the physician's finger or an iron rod pointing at them, they may possibly find good effects though they mistake the cause."

Franklin himself was in poor health, and too ill to attend the first examination of D'Eslon's methods. The other commissioners visited D'Eslon's clinic and watched in fascination and dismay as the mesmerized patients howled and shrieked and went into convulsions, and then became calm at the command of the "magnetizer."

They were not impressed with Mesmer's theories, though there was no denying the strange results. Examining the *baquet,* the commissioners found no elec-

26

tricity in the tub, and were unable to detect any sign of animal magnetism. They could not account for the strange screams and convulsions of D'Eslon's patients, however, and called forth more testing.

In April and May, the commissioners held tests at Franklin's house in Paris. They chose seven patients, neither lords nor ladies but ordinary working people. There were a boy with tuberculosis, a blind man, a widow troubled by asthma, a woman with a swelling on her thigh, and three others with varying ailments. Four out of the seven felt nothing at all when subjected to the streams of animal magnetism that supposedly flowed from D'Eslon's hands. The other three reported mild sensations of pain or discomfort. None were healed of their ills.

In June, the investigators held still more experiments on four people of higher social class. Two, Madame de Bory and M. Romagni, did not respond to the magnetic treatment. A third, M. Moret, who had a tumor on his knee, thought that it grew "warmer" when D'Eslon's hand passed over it. The fourth subject, Madame de V—, a victim of "nervous disorders," reacted more typically. She fell asleep during the treatment, that is, she was lulled by the magnetist's gestures into what we would call a hypnotic trance.

Franklin and his grandsons also let the magnetic doctor "magnetize" them. They felt no effect. Franklin, though, determined to get to the bottom of the phenomenon, devised a new experiment. He had D'Eslon magnet- 27 ize an apricot tree in the garden of his house, by direct-ing "magnetic fluid" toward it with his hands. According to D'Eslon, the tree would affect anyone who touched it.

A twelve-year-old boy was led forth, his eyes blind-folded. He was taken to four unmagnetized trees, one after another. The boy coughed and began to perspire as he touched the first tree. At the next, he complained of a headache. At the third tree, the headache grew worse. "I am getting closer to the magnetic tree," he declared, but actually he was heading away from it. When the boy reached the fourth tree, he fainted. But it was the excite-ment and attention that had overcome him, not the sup-posedly magnetized tree.

Mesmer had carefully remained on vacation during the months of these experiments. He had no wish for a face-to-face meeting with such men as the wise old Franklin, the keen-witted Lavoisier, and the brilliant Bailly. Late in the summer of 1784, he came back to Paris and was enthusiastically hailed by his followers. Money was collected for the establishment of schools of mesmerism—called "Societies of Harmony"—through-out France. Eager mesmerists contributed large sums of money.

Then, in August, the investigating commissioners made their report to King Louis. On September 4, Bailly read the report to the French Academy of Sciences. Franklin and his colleagues unanimously agreed that no

28 such thing as Mesmer's animal magnetism had been

shown to exist. They had seen no evidence at all of a "universal magnetic fluid."

What, then, had caused the convulsions and the rest of the effects?

They could all be explained simply enough, said the investigators. The patients were excited by the atmosphere of the sessions, by the hidden music, by the wand-waving and theatrical mummery. The contact with the hands of the magnetizers further stirred the patients to delirium. And since those who went to Mesmer *expected* to go into convulsions or hysteria, most of them actually did. It was the same sort of phenomenon that sometimes seizes a group of normal people and turns it into a howling, shrieking mob completely devoid of reason or order.

Mesmerism was dangerous, the commissioners declared. It was useless as medical treatment, and it could result in serious harm to the patients. They recommended that it be condemned and forbidden.

The report of the commissioners shattered Mesmer's reputation in France. The commission had not only included medical men—who might not have pure motives in condemning their eccentric rival Mesmer—but scientists, chemists, and astronomers, who had no professional axes to grind. Overnight, Mesmer's popularity evaporated. His mansion no longer swarmed with throngs of eager patients. He gathered up the profits of his seven years in Paris—340,000 francs—and retired from medical magnetism, eventually returning to his na- 29 tive Austria. He lived quietly there until his death in 1815, at the age of eighty-one.

Mesmer himself was out of the magnetizing business. But that did not spell the end of mesmerism. The magnetic "science" found a welcome in the United States, where Lafayette had been its most enthusiastic promoter. Thomas Jefferson denounced Mesmer as a "maniac," and called mesmerism a "compound of fraud and folly," but the Americans nevertheless were even more friendly to Mesmer's ideas than Paris had been.

One active mesmerist of the time was an American surgeon living in England, Benjamin Douglas Perkins. In 1798, Perkins took out a patent for "Metallic Tractors," nothing less than Father Hell's old idea, with which Mesmer had started his magnetic career. The "tractors" were steel plates which had been magnetized, and which Perkins said could cure gout, rheumatism, palsy, and just about everything else. The English bought Perkins' tractors in great numbers, at $25 a pair, and many miraculous cures were reported. Perkins was a Quaker, and the Society of Friends backed him heavily, building a hospital called the Perkinean Institution, where all might be treated with the magnetic plates.

Another doctor named Haygarth exploded the magnetic theory by treating patients with wooden plates painted to resemble steel. Wood could hardly be magnetized, but the patients responded just as well to the wooden plates as to the genuine ones. Haygarth published a pamphlet called "Of the Imagination as a Cause

30

and Cure of Disorders, exemplified by Fictitious Tractors." Perkins was laughed out of England, but he took
his plates and theories back to Pennsylvania and enjoyed great financial success there. His tractors had an
incredible sale in the early years of the nineteenth
century.

In France, where Mesmer himself no longer practiced, some of his followers continued magnetic research. While the commissioners were puncturing
Mesmer's theories in 1784, a wealthy nobleman, the
Marquis de Puysegur, was carrying out magnetic experiments at his country estate. He succeeded in putting a
young peasant into a deep hypnotic trance by telling him
that he felt "peace . . . peace . . . peace. . . ." Puysegur found that he could speak to the seemingly sleep-
ing man, get answers to his questions, and bring him out
of the trance at will.

Puysegur also spent a good deal of time magnetizing
elm trees, directing streams of magnetic fluid hither and
thither, and otherwise making use of the mythical trap-
pings of Mesmer's pseudoscience. But the Marquis was
on the right track when he realized that the most important aspect of animal magnetism was the ability to throw
the patient into a deep trance.

Another magnetizer of the 1780's, the Chevalier de
Barbarin, carried the theory a step further. He dis-
pensed with wands, *baquets,* and all other magnetic
paraphernalia. The magnetic sleep, he said, could be
achieved simply by speaking to the patient and imposing   31

one's will on him. No gadgets were necessary. Barbarin thus foreshadowed modern hypnotism.

In England, magnetism was in disgrace for a long while, thanks to Dr. Perkins. But a Scottish surgeon named James Braid took up the study in a serious way in the middle of the nineteenth century. Magnetism, Braid said, had nothing to do with these trances. He junked the whole theory of Mesmer and coined the word hypnotism, from the Greek *hypnos*, meaning "sleep." Braid thought that hypnotism had valuable medical uses. In his day, anesthesia was new and unreliable, and he felt that it was possible to shield patients from the pain of surgery by hypnotizing them.

Braid published a book called *Neurohypnology* in 1849. He was immediately denounced in his own country as a quack and a fraud, and was barred from the practice of medicine. But his book came to the notice of a French doctor named Liebault, who began using hypnotism on his patients. "All one has to do," Liebault wrote, "is to get the patient to look at your eyes or finger, and to quietly tell him that he is getting drowsy, and the hypnotic sleep will soon follow."

Hypnosis today is much more than a party stunt. Many surgeons use hypnosis as a substitute for anesthesia in cases where anesthetic drugs might jeopardize the patient's health. Women have painlessly given birth under hypnosis. Dentists have drawn teeth from hypnotized patients. Hypnosis has also proved valuable in 32 treatment of mental illness.

We still do not know why hypnosis works, or even what it really is. One hypnotist defines it as "an artificially induced state, usually (though not always) resembling sleep." Through the use of gestures, voice, or patterns of light, the hypnotist is able to lull the patient's mind into a sleeplike trance. The hypnotized patient is strangely sensitive to anything the hypnotist tells him: "You have just been splashed with a bucket of ice water," the hypnotist says, and the patient shivers and breaks out in gooseflesh!

So here we have the strange case of a hoax that turned out not to be a hoax after all. Mesmer himself was a shrewd operator in search of a fast franc. He took possession of a worthless medieval idea—the notion of a universal magnetic fluid—and turned it into a mystical healing method he called "animal magnetism." He concocted a fanciful and absurd theory and decked his salon out in bizarre decorations to impress his patients all the more. Then, clustering them around his tubs of supposedly magnetized water, Mesmer used the power of his personality to throw them into hypnotic trances.

Animal magnetism was sheer nonsense. Everything that Mesmer claimed was ridiculous and fraudulent. His methods were preposterous. Yet, buried beneath all the magical hocus-pocus, there was a kernel of scientific truth: hypnotism. Mesmer wrought better than he knew. There is perhaps no better instance of a hoaxing quack who helped to give the world something useful and beneficial.

33

3: The Men on the Moon

News traveled slowly in the world of a hundred thirty years ago—so slowly we can hardly imagine it now. Today, troops riot in the Congo and all the world knows of it by nightfall; a President speaks in Washington and television viewers in Paris and London and Vienna watch him speaking; an earthquake strikes in Chile and relief missions set out a few hours later.

It was not like that in 1835. Television, the radio, the
telephone, the telegraph—all were in the realm of fan-

tasy then. So were automobiles and airplanes. When news was made in Europe, it took weeks for the United States to learn of it. Something happening in Africa might not be known for months. When President Andrew Jackson signed a bill at the White House, a few days went by before anyone in such nearby cities as Philadelphia and New York found out about it.

In such a world, people depended heavily on their newspapers to inform them of current events—a "current event" being anything that had happened in recent weeks, months, or even years. One of the newest of the newspapers was the New York *Sun,* two years old in 1835. The *Sun* had some of the most talented reporters in the country, and in its short life had come to be widely respected. Its circulation was small, only some ten thousand copies a day, but by the standards of 1835 that was fairly healthy. (Today some of New York's newspapers sell half a million copies or more a day, and one paper sells several million.) The *Sun* did not look much like newspapers of today. It usually had only four pages in each issue, printed in eye-strainingly tiny type. There were no splashy headlines and no photographs. The reader who wanted to know the news simply read down one column and then down the next.

On August 25, 1835, the readers of the *Sun* were given a very startling story indeed. At long last, news of Sir John Herschel's scientific expedition to South Africa had reached the United States—and the *Sun* had a scoop on the story.

35

Herschel was one of the world's greatest astronomers. His father, Sir William Herschel, had been the leading astronomer of the eighteenth century; among his many achievements had been the discovery of the planet Uranus. William Herschel's only son, John, had no new planets to his credit, but he had carried out an important survey of the stars of the Northern Hemisphere. In 1833, he set out for Capetown, South Africa, to study the stars of the Southern Hemisphere. He and his family arrived on January 15, 1834, for a stay of several years. By March 4, Herschel was at work in his observatory at the Cape, and all the world waited for news of some remarkable astronomical discovery.

A year and a half later, the world was still waiting. Herschel, painstakingly making his observations, had sent no news home from South Africa. Then, in August of 1835, the New York *Sun* broke the long silence. On a Tuesday afternoon the *Sun* hit the streets with an account of Herschel's findings.

Herschel, it seemed, had trained a powerful new telescope on the moon—and had found life there! Trees and vegetation, oceans and beaches, bison and goats, cranes and pelicans—all this, and much more, could be seen on the face of earth's satellite! New York was agog with the astounding revelation.

The *Sun* showed great restraint in featuring the story. It made the front page, to be sure, over in the right-hand column. Instead of a bold, attention-getting headline, 36 there was the inconspicuous title:

GREAT ASTRONOMICAL DISCOVERIES
Lately Made by Sir John Herschel, LL.D., F.R.S., etc.
At the Cape of Good Hope

The *Sun* said that its articles were reprinted from "the supplement to the *Edinburgh Journal of Science*," published in Scotland. Seven articles in all ran in the *Sun*, and before the series had ended the young newspaper's circulation had boomed all the way up to 19,360 —making it the biggest-selling paper in the world.

The first installment said nothing about living creatures on the moon. It began in a wordy, old-fashioned way, speaking of "recent discoveries in Astronomy which will build an imperishable monument to the age in which we live, and confer upon the present generation of the human race a proud distinction through all future time." The rest of the first article told of Herschel's observatory at the Cape, speaking with authentic-sounding scientific detail about his various telescopes.

The remarkable new discoveries, it was stated, had been made with a revolutionary type of telescope. The best available telescope, according to Sir John, would allow him to view the moon as though from a distance of forty miles. That was not good enough. However, Herschel had devised a new telescope on boldly different optical principles. It cast an image on a screen, and a microscope could be used to magnify that image.

The trouble with this pretty theory is that it would not work; when such an image is magnified, it quickly be- 37 comes so faint that nothing at all can be seen. But the author of the article had a glib way of skipping over such difficulties or of burying them under a barrage of scientific-sounding words. Thus, the *Sun*'s readers learned, Herschel had found a method of "transfusing artificial light," thereby brightening the image. A "hydro-oxygen microscope" was used to show fine details.

The big telescope itself had a light-collecting lens twenty-four feet in diameter. (By way of comparison, the biggest telescope in use today, at California's Mount Palomar Observatory, has a two-hundred-inch mirror, that is, seventeen feet in diameter.) According to the *Sun*, the casting of the giant lens began on January 3, 1833, but after eight days of cooling it was found that the lens was flawed. The job had to be done over. The second lens was cast on January 27, and when examined early in February was found to be all but perfect. (It took years to cast and polish the mirror at the Mount Palomar Observatory.)

"The weight of this prodigious lens," the article said, "was 14,826 lbs., or nearly seven tons after being polished; and its estimated magnifying power [was] 42,000 times. It was therefore presumed to be capable of representing objects in our lunar satellite of little more than eighteen inches in diameter, provided its focal image of them could be rendered distinct by the transfusion of artificial light."

38   Herschel supposedly had sailed for Capetown with his

great lens on September 4, 1833. (Actually he left London on November 13.) The newspaper told how two teams of eighteen oxen each had hauled the lens to a high plateau, thirty-five miles northeast of Capetown, where Sir John set up his telescope. The observatory itself was described in the most minute detail; the author of the article studded his paragraphs with resounding and impressive terms and phrases like "angle of incidence," "focal distance," "theodolite," and so forth.

The patient reader, his curiosity aroused by this lengthy scientific preamble, at last got the first hint of what Herschel had seen. On January 10, 1834, Herschel had trained his vast telescope on the moon, the article declared. The microscope, when applied to the image from the telescope, revealed rocks of a vivid greenish-brown, and then clusters of a dark red flower, "precisely similar to the . . . rose-poppy of our cornfields." The delighted astronomer next gazed upon a lunar forest; the trees were evergreens, some resembling English yews, others "as fine a forest of firs, unequivocal firs, as I have ever seen cherished in the bosom of my native mountains."

New wonders followed: an ocean, bordered by "a beach of brilliant white sand," with high waves and deep-blue water. Then a strange district where "a lofty chain of obelisk-shaped, or very slender pyramids, standing in irregular groups, each composed of thirty or forty spires," could be seen. A twist of the fine adjustment   39 revealed that the obelisks were "monstrous amethysts, of a diluted claret color, glowing in the intensest light of the sun!"

Then came a barren desert of chalk and flint. Next, there swam into view a wild forest of oaklike and laurel-like trees, and at last the first lunar animal life to be seen—shaggy creatures much like bison. Soon Herschel spied a beast "of a bluish lead color, about the size of a goat, with a head and beard like him, and a *single horn*," and then pelicans, cranes, and other water birds wading for fish in a large river.

By this time, the readers of the *Sun* found it torment to wait for the next daily installment. The unicorn had provided a stunning climax for the second article; by the third day, newsboys were selling enormous quantities of the paper—as fast as they could get them to the streets.

There was much to gasp over on the third day. Palm trees with crimson flowers, bears with horns, reindeer and elk and moose, and a beaver-like animal that lacked a tail and walked on two feet—all this and more greeted the *Sun*'s readers. An island fifty-five miles long in a great sea offered geological miracles: "Its hills were pinnacled with tall quartz crystals, of so rich a yellow and orange hue that we at first supposed them to be pointed flames of fire." A miniature zebra, long-tailed birds like golden and blue pheasants, even lowly shell-fish on the shores, all were caught by Sir John's keen

telescopic eye.

The *Sun* had more revelations in the succeeding installments: cliffs with outcroppings of pure gold, a sheeplike animal with "an amazingly long neck" and "two long spiral horns, white as polished ivory," a romantic and beautiful wooded valley, and, in the fourth article, the paper actually announced the existence of men of the moon!

It was while peering at the wild valley that the astronomers "were thrilled with astonishment to perceive four successive flocks of large winged creatures, wholly unlike any kind of birds, descend with a slow, even motion from the cliffs on the western side, and alight upon the plain." When they landed, they folded their wings and walked like human beings, in a manner "both erect and dignified."

The newspaper declared that "they averaged four feet in height, were covered, except on the face, with short and glossy copper-colored hair, and had wings composed of a thin membrane, without hair, lying snugly upon their backs, from the top of the shoulders to the calves of the legs. The face, which was of a yellowish flesh color, was a slight improvement upon that of the large orang outang, being more open and intelligent. . . . In general symmetry of body and limbs they were infinitely superior to the orang outang. . . . The hair on the head was a darker color than that of the body, closely curled but apparently not woolly, and arranged in two curious semicircles over the temples of the forehead. Their feet could only be seen as they were alternately lifted in walking; but from what we could see of them in so transient a view they appeared thin and very protuberant at the heel. . . ."

The moon men with the batlike wings seemed to be engaged in conversation. Herschel saw them gesturing with hands and arms, as though talking. Before long, his telescope found the moon men swimming in a large lake, spreading their wings and shaking them duck-fashion to rid them of water when they emerged. At length, the "man-bats," as Herschel supposedly dubbed them, flew off into the darkness and were lost to view.

Further telescopic exploration located a temple in a lovely setting, rimmed by hills "either of snow-white marble or semi-transparent crystal, we could not distinguish which." The temple itself was three-sided, "built of polished sapphire, or of some resplendent blue stone, which, like it, displayed a myriad points of golden light twinkling and scintillating in the sunbeams."

Later, other temples of equal beauty were discovered. No one, though, seemed to visit them except flocks of wild doves. The author of the *Sun*'s article wondered, "Had the devotees of these temples gone the way of all living, or were the latter merely historical monuments?" He hoped that one day an answer would be forthcoming, as further lunar study progressed.

Near one of the temples more moon men were sighted, "of a larger stature than the former specimens, less dark in color, and in *every respect* an improved variety of 42 the race." The penetrating eye of the telescope revealed them as they ate a large yellow fruit like a gourd, ripping away the rind with their fingers and gobbling the meat avidly. Then, too, they could be seen sucking the juice of a smaller red fruit. "They seemed eminently happy, and even polite, for we saw, in many instances, individuals sitting nearest these piles of fruit, select the largest and brightest specimens, and throw them archwise across the circle to some opposite friend. . . ."

It seemed that the moon men never engaged in any activity but "collecting various fruits in the woods, eating, flying, bathing, and loitering about on the summits of precipices." In the kindly, fertile environment of the moon, labor and industry were unnecessary. Nor was there war or weapons, apparently, though fire was known.

Fire caused trouble for the astronomers on earth. One night, so the *Sun* related, a careless assistant failed to lower the great lens. Morning sunrise struck the lens; a beam of light was hurled against the side of the observatory, burning a hole fifteen feet in circumference, and "so fierce was the concentration of the solar rays through the gigantic lens, that a clump of trees standing in a line with them was set on fire." Here the scientifically knowledgeable author of the article made a slip, for anyone who has ever used a magnifying glass to start a fire knows that a lens concentrates sunlight into a point, never in a line. But no one seemed to be troubled by this statement in the *Sun*.

It took a week, the readership learned, to repair the damage. By that time, the moon was not visible, and so   43 the astronomers turned their attention to Saturn. The rings of that planet, they discovered, were "the fragments of two destroyed worlds, formerly belonging to our solar system"—an opinion that modern astronomers would not find seriously objectionable. But these rings, "the skeletons of former globes," the *Sun* said, "were not devoid of mountains and seas."

The last of the seven articles trailed off in vague observations of other planets, and then returned briefly to the moon for a last look at a new tribe of moon men, "of infinitely greater personal beauty" than the others, very much like the angels of "the more imaginative schools of painters." The *Sun* concluded the series by informing the readers that forty pages of mathematical calculations, which had accompanied the original articles in the *Edinburgh Journal of Science*, would not be reprinted here because of their extreme difficulty and lack of popular appeal.

The *Sun* series caused a sensation. It was an age when scientists were making wonderful new discoveries constantly, and when very little was known about the surface of the moon. Here were scientific-sounding articles declaring that the moon was a veritable paradise, with wooded glades, streams and rivers, and handsome winged men and women. Sir John Herschel himself was the authority for this, was he not? Who could question Sir John's statements?

The other newspapers were quick to comment on the astounding revelations, and on September 1, 1835, the

Sun proudly printed excerpts from their editorials. "Sir John has added a stock of knowledge to the present age that will immortalize his name," said the *Daily Advertiser*, an Albany paper that regarded the discovery with "unspeakable emotions of pleasure and astonishment." The New York *Times* offered the opinion that "the writer displays the most extensive and accurate knowledge of astronomy. . . . The accounts of the wonderful discoveries in the moon, etc., are all probable and plausible." The *New Yorker*, no relative of today's magazine of that name, hailed "a new era in astronomy and science generally."

Two Yale professors named Olmstead and Loomis hurried down from New Haven to confer with the editor of the *Sun*, Benjamin Day. They were excited by the story, and wanted to see the original Edinburgh articles, with those forty pages of mathematical calculations. The editor referred them to a reporter named Richard Adams Locke, who stalled them awhile, then told them that the articles were at the *Sun*'s printshop. The professors set out for the printer, but Locke sent a messenger ahead of them, instructing the printer to send them somewhere else. Olmstead and Loomis were shunted from office to office all day, and, finally, without getting to see the calculations, gave up and returned to Yale.

The *Journal of Commerce*, a distinguished rival newspaper, was so taken with the moon story that it wanted permission to reprint it as a separate pamphlet. A *Journal of Commerce* man paid a call on *Sun* editor Day, 45 and was also sent to see Richard Adams Locke. Locke tried to talk the man out of reprinting the articles. He gave no reason at first, simply suggesting it might do the *Journal of Commerce*'s reputation no good to put out the pamphlet. Finally Locke broke down and told his fellow reporter the truth: the entire moon story was a hoax.

Herschel had never found life on the moon, neither unicorns nor bat men nor two-legged beavers. He had no twenty-four-foot telescope lens, no "hydro-oxygen microscope." The details of the story were purely imaginary. What's more, Locke revealed, the *Edinburgh Journal of Science* had gone out of business several years before, and therefore this series could not have been, and was not, a reprint. He, Richard Adams Locke, one of the New York *Sun*'s cleverest and most able reporters, had invented the whole business.

The following day the *Journal of Commerce* printed Locke's confession and gleefully denounced the supposed Herschel discoveries for the hoax they were. The *Sun*, which had run the articles as a stunt to build circulation, saw a chance to keep the fun alive. The paper denied that Locke had ever admitted anything to the *Journal of Commerce* man. Every paper in the country, the *Sun* said, had praised the articles. But the *Journal of Commerce* was an exception, "because it not only ignorantly doubted the authenticity of the discoveries, but ill-naturedly said that we had fabricated them for the purpose of making a noise and drawing attention to our
46   paper."

Keeping their faces straight, the editors and reporters of the *Sun* went on insisting for another two weeks that the moon story was honest. Then, on September 16, 1835, the *Sun* finally confessed to the hoax in print. The newspaper-reading public sorrowfully came to realize that the wonderful forests and lakes of the moon did not exist.

Locke had written a brilliant science-fiction story, and the *Sun* had slyly passed it off as fact. The reporter's poetic style, his clear description, and above all his confident use of scientific language, had made the hoax vividly realistic. It has been claimed that he received technical assistance from a French astronomer named Jean Nicolas Nicollet, then living in New York, or from one Dr. Dick, author of a work on means of communicating with the moon. Locke himself maintained that he had written the articles without help. His grand hoax is a good key to the state of popular scientific knowledge in the United States in the year 1835. So very little was known about the moon that it was not at all difficult for the glib and extremely plausible hoax to win thousands of believers.

The *Sun* made itself famous through the hoax. For years afterward, the lively, sensational, cent-a-copy newspaper was one of the most successful in New York. Nine years after the moon hoax, it worked the same stunt again, running an article headlined, "Astounding News by Express via Norfolk; the Atlantic Crossed in Three Days; Signal Triumph of Mr. Monck's Flying Machine." This fantastic tale of an imaginary balloon flight stirred wide excitement until its falsity was revealed. (The author of the article, by the way, was a penniless young writer named Edgar Allan Poe.)

Richard Adams Locke went on to fashion an outstanding career in journalism. A few months after the moon hoax, Locke was involved in another hoax, not as hoaxer but as exposer. P. T. Barnum, the great circus impresario, had been exhibiting an old Negro woman named Joice Heth, who was, so Barnum claimed, one hundred and sixty-one years old and who had been the nurse of the infant George Washington in the 1730's. When Joice Heth died in 1836, Locke attended the autopsy. The verdict of the doctors who examined her body was that she was at best eighty years old, and therefore she could not possibly have been Washington's nurse. Locke exposed Barnum's hoax the next day in an article in the *Sun.*

Another paper promptly challenged him. The New York *Herald* called Locke's article on the Joice Heth autopsy "nothing more than a complete hoax from beginning to end." The *Herald* reminded the readers how Locke had deliberately fooled New York the previous summer with his moon hoax. Then the *Herald* proceeded to concoct a hoax of its own. The autopsy, it claimed, had not been performed on the real Joice Heth at all, but on a Harlem woman known only as Aunt Nelly. Joice Heth, it was stated, was still on exhibit in Connecticut.

A few months later, the *Herald* finally broke the tangled web of hoax and counterhoax by admitting that Locke's original story had actually been true. Joice Heth was really dead, and she had not been one hundred and sixty-one years old when she died. Stories such as this seem representative of the state of American journalism in the 1830's.

As for Sir John Herschel, whose good name had been dragged into the moon story, he remained in South Africa carrying out important scientific observations until 1838. His report on the work, not published until 1847, said nothing at all about bat-winged men on the moon.

Herschel eventually learned of Locke's hoax. The news got to South Africa in 1836 or 1837, and the great astronomer thought it was a very funny story. Herschel was also amused to get a letter from a group of Baptist clergymen in the United States. They congratulated him heartily on his discovery of life on the moon, and informed him that they had held "prayer meetings for the benefit of brethren in the newly explored regions." The clergymen beseeched Sir John to tell them "whether science affords any prospects of a method of conveying the Gospel to residents in the moon."

We do not know what answer Herschel made to the good gentlemen of the clergy. Perhaps he gently broke the news to them that the moon is a dead world, airless and waterless, not at all suitable to a missionary operation. To this day, no one has brought the Gospel to the 49 winged people of the moon. In a few years astronauts and cosmonauts will head moonward for the first manned landings on our gleaming companion in space—and the odds are very much against their finding the unicorns and bat men that dazzled our believing great-great-great-grandfathers in the summer of 1835.

4: The Sea Serpent
of Dr. Koch

The Apollo Rooms, an exhibition hall at 410 Broadway in New York City, was the scene of an extraordinary display in the summer of 1845. For twenty-five cents, no small amount when a dollar was a good day's wage, curiosity-seekers could view a majestic sea serpent 114 feet long, whose mounted skeleton weighed 7,500 pounds.

This splendid creature was the property of one Dr. Albert Koch, who had found the fossilized skeleton in Alabama in March. He called it Hydrarchus, or some-   51 times Hydrargos, meaning "water king" in Greek. Hydrarchus, Dr. Koch asserted, was the monster known in the Bible as Leviathan. "None is so fierce that dare stir him up," said the Book of Job. "Out of his nostrils goeth smoke, as out of a seething pot or caldron. . . . Upon earth there is not his like."

The public was passionately interested in sea serpents, and people came in great numbers to look at Dr. Koch's Hydrarchus. For centuries, men had speculated about the monsters of the deep. The Roman naturalist Pliny had told of sea serpents thirty feet long that had caused problems for a Greek exploring squadron at sea in the Persian Gulf. Olaus Magnus, Archbishop of Uppsala, set down a description in 1555 of a sea serpent two hundred feet long and twenty feet thick seen off the Norwegian coast. "This snake . . . puts up his head on high like a pillar, and catcheth away men, and he devours them," Olaus wrote.

Nearly two centuries later another Scandinavian clergyman, Hans Egede of Norway, encountered a sea serpent while on a missionary journey to Greenland. He wrote: "Anno 1734, July. On the 6th appeared a very terrible sea-animal, which raised itself so high above the water, that its head reached above our maintop. It had a long, sharp snout, and blew like a whale, had broad, large flappers, and the body was, as it were, covered with a hard skin, and it was very wrinkled and uneven on its skin; moreover on the lower part it was formed like a snake, and when it went under water again, it cast itself backwards, and in doing so it raised its tail above the water, a whole ship-length from its body. That evening we had very bad weather."

Egede was considered a reliable witness. So was Commander Lorenz von Ferry, who swore in 1746 that he had seen a sea serpent whose head, "which it held more than two feet above the surface of the water, resembled that of a horse. . . . It had large black eyes and a long white mane, which hung down to the surface of the water. Besides the head and neck, we saw seven or eight folds, or coils, of this snake, which were very thick, and as far as we could guess there was a fathom's distance between each fold." When von Ferry fired his gun in the air, the serpent vanished into the depths.

From New England came the next report, of a "strange marine animal" eighty to ninety feet long, and about the width "of a half-barrel." This beast turned up in the harbor of Gloucester, Cape Ann, about thirty miles from Boston. In the spring of 1817, a scholarly group, the Linnaean Society of New England, appointed a three-man commission to look into the matter. The commissioners interviewed the sailors who claimed to have seen the monster. Everyone agreed that the creature was limbless and snakelike, with a row of humps down its back.

The investigators turned in a sober report, concluding that something mysterious had indeed been swimming off Gloucester that year. This led a certain Captain Richard Rich to put to sea toward the end of 1817 with the 53 intention of capturing the Gloucester serpent and bringing it back to Boston for exhibit. Failing to find the monster, Captain Rich hauled in a large tuna fish and exhibited its bones in a dime show, claiming that it was the sea serpent. He fooled very few, and quickly admitted his deception. In 1818, another New England skipper, Captain Joseph Woodward, came back to port with word of a huge sea serpent that had pursued his ship at an incredible speed for more than five hours. Captain Woodward had tried to frighten the creature away with musket fire, and even with cannon shots, but it was undisturbed by the artillery and nearly carried the ship to destruction before Captain Woodward managed to elude it.

No one had ever explained away these various sea serpents. And so, although it had been many years since the last sighting of one, the public was still keenly interested in the whole sea-serpent idea when Dr. Koch produced his impressive 114-foot-long skeleton.

It was a magnificent and majestic sight. On and on it stretched, a fossil almost forty yards long, a vast length of bleached bones. It was long but narrow, snakelike, with small paddlelike limbs. Who could fail to experience a chill of awe, beholding this prehistoric creature? Who could not agree that this must be some ancient cousin of the monsters sighted by Hans Egede, Lorenz von Ferry, and Joseph Woodward?

Certain unromantic scientists failed to share Koch's 54 enthusiasm for Hydrarchus. They came to the Apollo

Rooms, they pondered the huge skeleton, and they offered their coldly rational opinion.

Dr. Koch's sea serpent, they declared, was nothing but a shameless fraud. The mighty Hydrarchus had been assembled, they insisted, from the bones of at least five separate animals. Koch had magnified his monster greatly by cunningly adding extra ribs and vertebrae. "These remains never belonged to one and the same animal," declared the zoologist Jeffries Wyman. Nor was Hydrarchus even a real serpent. "The anatomical characteristics of the teeth," Wyman wrote, "indicate that they are not those of a reptile but of a warm blooded mammal."

Dr. Koch protested. It was in vain, for Dr. Koch was well known to the scientific world. This was not the first time he had used his imagination in reconstructing fossil bones. He was already notorious.

German-born Albert Koch had come to America about 1835. If he had any scientific training in his homeland, he never mentioned it to anyone, but when he arrived in the United States he set himself up as a dealer in fossil specimens. Using St. Louis as his headquarters, Koch roamed much of the southern part of the United States, digging up old bones, putting them on exhibit, and selling them to museums when the paying public began to lose interest in the displays.

This commercial approach to fossil-hunting did not endear Koch to scientists. The first half of the nineteenth   55 century was a time of eager fossil-finding, animal after extinct animal being rediscovered, and the men who were doing the work objected to Koch's profiteering ways. Science was science, they said, and moneymaking was moneymaking, and the two should not be mixed.

Koch ignored the wagging fingers and went on peddling old bones. Early in 1840, he unearthed an imposing skeleton in Benton County, Missouri. It was that of the extinct elephant known as the mastodon, which had roamed North America widely until about ten thousand years ago.

Mastodon bones had been found in New England in the seventeenth century—the Puritan preacher Cotton Mather had identified them as "the thighbones of giants" who had lived before the Deluge—and when a four-pound mastodon tooth was unearthed, Mather declared it was probably human. More mastodon bones were found in the eighteenth century, and were correctly seen to be those of an elephant rather than of giant men.

Koch knew that he had found a mastodon's bones. They lay on the shore of a small Missouri river, the Pomme de Terre, covered over with clay, gravel, and quicksand. Koch's report on the excavation indicates that he took considerable pains to do the job scientifically; he made careful geological records of the types of soil in which the fossil lay, and even noted the well-preserved vegetable matter surrounding the skeleton. "All of the vegetable remains," he wrote, "are tropical or very low southern production. They consisted of large quantities of cypress burs, wood and bark; a great deal of tropical cane and tropical swamp moss"; and other plant forms now found only well to the south. Evidently Missouri's climate was much milder when mastodons flourished there.

He was not nearly as scientific when he set about assembling the scattered bones of his mastodon. With an eye toward impressing the public, Koch put the skeleton together in the most dramatic possible way. He mounted the curved tusks, which were enormous, on top of the head so that they jutted upward like gigantic horns. Finding the bones of more than one mastodon at the site, Koch wove them all together into one truly jumbo specimen, which would have been a colossus among beasts if it had ever really existed.

Koch now proceeded to haul this awe-inspiring horned mastodon all over the country on an exhibition tour. He dubbed it Missourium, as though to set it apart from the mastodons already known, which bore the scientific name of *Mastodon americanus*. By October, 1841, Koch was in Philadelphia with this Missourium, and put it on display at the Masonic Hall.

The American Philosophical Society, the venerable scientific association founded by Benjamin Franklin in 1743, heard a discussion of Koch's Missourium on October 15, 1841. Dr. Richard Harlan, one of America's leading authorities on fossils, told the society that "There is now exhibiting at the Masonic Hall in Philadelphia, one of the most extensive and remarkable col-   57 lections of fossil bones of extinct mammals which have hitherto been brought to light in this country." Dr. Harlan praised "the perseverance of the enterprising proprietor, Mr. Albert Koch of St. Louis, Missouri." Tactfully, Dr. Harlan observed that Koch had made certain strange errors in mounting the mastodon skeleton, such as attaching the tusks upside-down to form horns, but declared that "no doubt" Koch's later research "would enable him to rectify these errors."

Cheered by his enthusiastic reception by the American Philosophical Society, Koch moved along, circus-fashion, to show his collection elsewhere. By the end of the year, this Barnum of old bones had turned up in London, and Missourium went on display at Egyptian Hall in Piccadilly just before Christmas, 1841.

One of the many Londoners who came out to see it was Richard Owen, the well-known anatomist and pale-ontologist. Owen was skeptical, to put it mildly, about the way Koch had assembled the mastodon, and said so in a paper read to the Geological Society of London. Not at all awed by Owen's reputation, Koch appeared before the same body a few months later to defend his position. Meanwhile, Egyptian Hall was crowded with paying customers. Not until the summer of 1843 did Koch take his fossils on tour again. He showed them in Dublin, then traveled through Europe with them, ending his wanderings in his native Germany. Berlin was as excited by the fearsome Missourium as London and Dublin had

58   been.

In May, 1844, Koch started back toward the United States. Stopping off in London, he lightened his baggage by selling the skeleton of Missourium to the British Museum for a staggering price: two thousand dollars as a down payment, plus one thousand dollars a year for the rest of his life. (He collected twenty-three thousand dollars under this arrangement before his death in 1866.) As soon as the grotesque fossil had changed hands, British Museum paleontologists began stripping it of its extra bones and putting the tusks where they belonged. When they were finished, Missourium—rechristened *Mastodon americanus*—looked less sensational but very much more probable. The dehorned mastodon is still to be seen in the Fossil Mammal Gallery of the British Museum; indeed, it is one of the finest mastodon fossils in existence.

Having peddled his prime attraction, Koch now needed a new money-maker, and he swiftly found one. March of 1845 saw him in Alabama, unearthing the remains of his "gigantic fossil reptile," Hydrarchus. Koch spent most of that spring piecing Hydrarchus together out of a generous supply of bones, and in the summer he brought it to New York for public display.

Koch published a descriptive pamphlet to be sold at the exhibit. On the front page, he gave himself the title of "Dr." Koch, and as Dr. Koch he thenceforth was known, though he never explained what he had done to merit the designation. Dr. Koch also invented a scientific name for his sea serpent: *Hydrarchus sillimani.* The name honored Benjamin Silliman, a famous Yale professor.

Such a name left Koch open to the shafts of skeptical punsters. "It would be a *silly man* indeed who believed in *Hydrarchus sillimani*," one critic said. Dr. Silliman himself was not at all pleased to have his name attached to such a weird and fraudulent creature, and he asked Koch to remove it forthwith.

Koch obliged. He renamed the sea serpent *Hydrarchus harlani*, this time honoring Dr. Harlan of Philadelphia, who had praised him in 1841. It was a safe choice, for Harlan had died in 1843, and could raise no objections.

Objections aplenty were raised by living paleontologists. One scientist pointed out that Hydrarchus was not a newly discovered species at all. A very similar, though of course smaller, fossil had been found in 1842, and Dr. Harlan himself had given it the name of *Basilosaurus cetoides*, "the whale-like king lizard." Ten years before that, Richard Owen of England had studied another specimen, which he identified (correctly) as a seagoing mammal. Owen gave his gigantic specimen the name Zeuglodon.

The creature described by Owen and by Harlan had been impressive enough, fifty to sixty feet long but only about eight feet thick. Zeuglodon had had four feet of head, ten feet of body, and more than forty feet of tail, ending in great flukes like those of a whale. It must have

looked very serpentlike as it thrashed through the water,

except for the tiny paddlelike flippers just back of the head. But it was warm-blooded, no serpent at all.

Dr. Koch had whipped up a fantastic super-Zeuglodon, twice the real length of the creature, and it drew huge crowds to the Apollo Rooms. The public took little notice of the carping of the scientists. The strongest attack came from the Boston zoologist Jeffries Wyman, who was the first to observe that Koch had strung together vertebrae from at least five Zeuglodons to form his Hydrarchus. Wyman also pointed out that some of the "bones" in Hydrarchus' flippers were actually the fossilized shells of a mollusk similar to the *Nautilus*. In short, Wyman concluded that the great sea serpent which had been "discovered" by Dr. Koch was a hoax and an absurdity.

Wyman read his devastating paper before the Boston Society of Natural History in October, 1845. It happened that Dr. Koch and the Hydrarchus were in Boston at the same time, though Koch apparently did not attend the meeting at which he was attacked. Another distinguished visitor to Boston that month was the English geologist Charles Lyell, who was making a tour of the United States. Lyell later had this to say about Koch and his fossil:

"During the first part of my stay in Boston, October, 1845, we one day saw the walls in the principal streets covered with placards, in which the words SEA SERPENT ALIVE figured conspicuously. On approaching near enough to read the smaller type of this advertisement, I found that Mr. Koch was about to exhibit to the Bostonians the fossil skeleton of 'that colossal and terrible reptile the *sea serpent,* which, when *alive,* measured thirty feet in circumference.' The public was also informed that this hydrarchus, or water king, was the leviathan of the Book of Job, chapter xli."

Lyell doubted Koch's opinion that his monster had been a seagoing reptile. He preferred Wyman's view that Hydrarchus had been a mammal. In February, 1846, Lyell carried out some further investigations into Koch's activities while touring Alabama. He visited the spot where Koch said he had found Hydrarchus, and talked to some of the local inhabitants. Yes, they said, Koch had dug up bones here, but he had dug up similar bones all over the area—including some vertebrae from "Washington County, fifteen miles distant in a direct line from this place, where the head was discovered." It was proof, as though any were really needed, that Koch had assembled his monstrosity out of many different specimens.

Lyell wrote to Benjamin Silliman on February 4, 1846, relaying the truth about Koch, but the clever doctor was once again on the high seas, heading for Europe to dazzle the curious. He got a frosty reception in London, where his Missourium hoax was still well remembered. The public had had a chance to see the mastodon in its proper form, and no longer trusted Koch's spectacular fossils. Dr. Gideon A. Mantell, a British paleon-

tologist, sent a letter to the *Illustrated London News* that let the public know what Americans such as Wyman were saying about the sea serpent.

Mantell pointed out that "Mr. Koch is the person who, a few years ago, had a fine collection of fossil bones of elephants and mastodons, out of which he made up an enormous skeleton, and exhibited it in the Egyptian Hall, Piccadilly, under the name of 'Missourium.' This collection was purchased by the trustees of the British Museum and from it were selected the bones which now constitute the skeleton of the Mastodon. . . ."

Germany was more friendly. Hydrarchus made a big hit in Berlin, and scored a public triumph in Dresden. An important German anatomist, C. G. Carus, made a special study of the sea serpent, publishing it in 1847. Carus was convinced that Hydrarchus was genuine. His report impressed King Frederick Wilhelm IV, who bought the monster for the collection of the Royal Museum in Berlin. Once again, Koch had reaped a handsome financial reward for his labors. More traveling salesman than scientist, he profited nicely from his European tour of 1846–47.

Koch had found a good way to make a living. By July, 1847, he was back in Alabama, searching for another Hydrarchus, and the following winter he uncovered a useful fossil in Washington County. Once again he assembled it—this new Hydrarchus was not quite as huge as the first, but it was awesome enough—and took it on tour. He displayed it in Dresden, Germany, in 1849; after that his track becomes uncertain, until he 63 bobs up again exhibiting his sea serpent in New Orleans four years later. (This second Hydrarchus eventually was destroyed in the Chicago Fire of 1871. The first one, minus its extra bones, is now kept at the University of Berlin.)

It seems that Koch eventually wearied of the circus life he was leading. He returned to St. Louis and settled down permanently. He became a member of the newly founded Academy of Science of St. Louis, and in 1857 was appointed chairman of its committee on comparative anatomy. For the remaining nine years of his life, Koch lived quietly, made wealthy by his career as an exhibitor of gaudy fossil monsters. At his death, he was regarded in St. Louis as an important scientist, but most respectable men of science considered him a shameless hoaxer.

There is one really tragic aspect to this story, for, before he began putting horns on mastodons and stringing extra vertebrae onto his sea serpent, Koch did make one scientific discovery of first-rate importance. It was a discovery that could have won him a glorious place in the history of science. But no one believed him, because by the time this discovery was announced Koch had already established his reputation as a peddler of phony fossils.

It happened in October, 1838. A farmer in Gasconade County, Missouri, was engaged in digging a well near
his house when he came upon some large animal bones,

a stone knife, and an Indian axe. News of the discovery reached St. Louis, where Koch was living, and he hurried to the scene.

The bones found by the farmer had broken into fragments when he dug them up. Koch, however, began to excavate, and soon found new remains. His first account of the discovery appeared in the January 12, 1839, issue of *The Presbyterian*, a weekly newspaper published in Philadelphia.

This story told how, below layers of clay and sand, he came upon more bones, axes of a curious type, and spearpoints similar to well-known Indian points. All about "was ashes nearly from six inches to one foot in depth, intermixed with burned wood and burned bones, broken spears, axes, knives, etc." A large animal had evidently become mired in mud and clay, been killed by Indians, and been roasted and eaten on the spot. "The fire appeared to have been the largest on the head and neck of the animal, as the ashes and coals were much deeper here than in the rest of the body; the skull was quite perfect, but so much burned, that it crumbled to dust on the least touch."

This was a discovery of major significance. No one then had any idea how long man had lived in North America. It was generally believed that the Indians had crossed out of Asia via the narrow Bering Strait, and had migrated down through Alaska and Canada into what is now the United States. (This is still the accepted theory.) But how long ago had they come here? Many scientists felt that the migration had taken place quite recently by archaeological standards, say, ten or fifteen centuries ago.

It was well known that long ago North America had had a near-tropical climate, and had been inhabited by such warm-weather animals as elephants, rhinoceroses, and giant ground sloths. These big creatures had all become extinct in North America many thousands of years before. If someone could discover evidence that man had been here then, had hunted and killed these ancient beasts, it would prove that the theorists of a recent migration were wrong.

Now, in 1838, Albert Koch had found that evidence: the charred skeleton of an extinct beast, associated with spears and axes. Koch thought that the animal had been a mastodon, whereas it appears that it really was a giant ground sloth, but the main point is the same in either case. Mastodons and ground sloths both were long since extinct.

Why Koch chose to publish his report in *The Presbyterian,* no one knows. All articles printed in that paper were unsigned, so he could not even claim credit for his find. Benjamin Silliman of Yale came across the article in the spring of 1839, and was so excited by it that he reprinted it in *The American Journal of Science and Arts,* calling it "interesting and important." Silliman asked that "the unknown author communicate with us directly."

66 Doubtless Koch was unaware of Silliman's request, or

he would have stepped forward to announce himself as that unknown author, since we know he was fond of publicity. Perhaps he was too busy unearthing fossils to read Silliman's magazine. In 1840, Koch put together his first large collection of fossils and sold them to a group in Philadelphia, who gave them to the American Philosophical Society. Then, returning to Missouri, he found the fossil mastodon he called Missourium, and began his career of creating supermonsters.

In the summer of 1841, while exhibiting Missourium in Louisville, Kentucky, Koch once again described his 1838 find, in a pamphlet headed "Evidence of Human Existence Contemporary with Fossil Animals." He described his excavation in detail, giving a clear and scientific account of everything he had done. And he added one bit of evidence that had not been in his earlier report:

"There was embedded immediately under the femur, or hind leg bone of this animal, an arrowhead of rose colored flint, resembling those used by the American Indians, but of larger size. This was the only arrowhead immediately with the skeleton; but in the same strata at a distance of five or six feet, in a horizontal direction, four more arrowheads were found; three of these were of the same formation as the preceding; the fourth was of very rude workmanship. One of the last mentioned three was of agate, the others of blue flint. These arrowheads are indisputably the work of human hands. I examined the deposit in which they were embedded, and 67 raised them out of their embedment with my own hands."

Koch's flamboyant exploits with Missourium and Hydrarchus had ruined his never very sturdy scientific reputation. The authorities who read his reports spoke of his "want of accuracy" and "lively imagination," and laughed him out of court. They declared that Koch was simply a promoter who sold entertainment to a gullible public. How could such a man be taken seriously?

Decades went by. To the end of his life, Koch continued to publish reports defending his arrowhead-and-charred-bones discovery. No one supported him. Half a dozen times during the late nineteenth century, other men found human relics associated with mastodon and ground sloth remains, but these were brushed aside the same way. The official scientific position was that mankind had come to the New World about the time of Christ, certainly no earlier than that. The leading experts on American prehistory insisted that no human beings had ever hunted mastodons in North America.

In 1926, J. D. Figgins of the Denver Museum of Natural History excavated a site eight miles west of the town of Folsom, New Mexico, and came upon the bones of another extinct mammal, a type of large bison. Embedded in the clay surrounding one bone was an unusual arrowhead, about two inches long, with a narrow groove carved down its face. Figgins immediately concluded that he had found proof that man and this bison had 68 been contemporaries in ancient New Mexico.

Figgins was a respected archaeologist, and no one accused him of hoaxing. Yet the authorities trotted forth the same arguments they had been using in such cases for decades. The arrowhead, they said, was "intrusive," that is, it was younger than the bison fossil, and had worked its way down into the earth, perhaps buried by some busy squirrel. The experts refused to accept Figgins' discovery as proof of anything.

The next year, he dug again at the same site, and again found bison and arrowheads. This time the point was lodged *between the ribs* of a bison! Three of the eastern authorities journeyed to New Mexico, examined the evidence, and agreed that Figgins had undoubtedly found something. Now there was indisputable proof that men had hunted these bison long ago.

Figgins holds the credit for making the first positive discovery of this sort. He pushed man's existence in North America back at least ten thousand years, and many archaeologists today believe that men reached the New World as early as thirty thousand years ago. No one today cries "hoax!" when charred mastodon remains are found associated with arrow or spearpoints.

But what of Koch, and his pioneering find? He gets no credit at all. He was only a charlatan, after all. But there is no reason to think he was hoaxing in this case. There was no profit in it for him, and, since he published his first report anonymously, he did not even seem to want fame. His reports on the Gasconade County find are sober, serious, and detailed. We know today, thanks to 69

Figgins' find and others, that it is perfectly possible for Koch to have made such a discovery.

Koch is in the sad position of the boy who cried "wolf" once too often. He might have been known today as an important figure in the story of American archaeology. Instead—thanks to his fondness for cash and public acclaim—he is chiefly remembered as the man who built a sea serpent and a mastodon with horns.

5: John Keely's
Perpetual-Motion Machine

It's a universal human desire to want to get something for nothing. Unfortunately, just about everything worthwhile turns out to have some sort of price tag—especially the power needed to run a motor.

That hasn't stopped inventors from trying, for a good many centuries now, to get something for nothing by inventing a so-called perpetual-motion machine. Such a machine is not intended to go on moving forever, as the name might imply. Rather, its purpose is to do useful

71

work without drawing on an external energy source, or, at the very least, to give off more energy than is needed to run it.

Modern physics casts a very doubtful eye on such an enterprise. The first law of thermodynamics holds that it's impossible to create energy, and no one has yet managed to find a loophole in that law. Such seeming perpetual-motion machines as have been built all turn out to have some secret power source, or to be drawing on energy in some way that even the inventor perhaps does not realize.

The laws of thermodynamics, though, are simply the result of centuries of observation. They report on the nature of things, but they are not universal laws handed down by some infallible authority. Many clever men have entertained sneaking hopes that there might somewhere be an exception to them.

Most of the early perpetual-motion machines depended on gravity to generate energy. One type consisted of a closed wheel divided by spokes into compartments, each compartment containing a weighted ball. The idea was that once the wheel was given a starting push, the weight of the balls would keep it turning indefinitely. Eventually, though, energy lost through friction tends to slow the wheel down and halt it—requiring another push to start the wheel going again. Not very productive!

As early as the thirteenth century, a Parisian architect observed, "Many a time have skilful workmen tried to contrive a wheel that shall turn of itself," and he suggested a way to do it by weighting it with quicksilver or with "an uneven number of mallets." Leonardo da Vinci apparently experimented along these lines several hundred years later, without results. In the seventeenth century, the Marquis of Worcester built an elaborate wheel fourteen feet across, weighted by metal balls of fifty pounds apiece. A German inventor a century later constructed a similar device, but in neither case was perpetual motion achieved.

A mill turned by waterpower is a classic producer of energy. The mill will only turn so long as the millstream is flowing; in order to get energy out of the system, energy must go in, and if the stream runs dry, the mill stops. A number of inventors tackled the problem of constructing a recycling mill system; water would run past the mill's wheel, making it turn, and then somehow would be lifted back to its starting point to turn the wheel again. Alas, the lifting process required energy too, and so the inventors who tried to build such installations found that they were out of luck so far as free energy was concerned.

Many other ingenious-sounding gadgets were designed, based on this principle and that, in the eighteenth and nineteenth centuries. All of them foundered on the same point. No matter what method was used to keep the motor going, that method demanded energy in some fashion. Every one of these perpetual motion machines required an energy input.

73

Then a clever Yankee named John Worrell Keely came along in 1872 and showed the world how it could be done.

Keely proposed to use the energy of atoms as his power source. Nobody in 1872, least of all Keely, knew anything about the phenomenon we call radioactivity, which makes possible the release of energy from heavy elements like uranium. He meant to draw energy from simpler, more easily available substances—such as water.

All atoms, Keely said, were in constant vibration. (Which is true, by the way.) The trick was to harness and channel this random vibration. Keely claimed to be able to make the atoms in a given substance vibrate together, in unison. He could then draw on the "etheric force" of these vibrating atoms to run any motor of any size.

In 1872, Keely began to seek funds for his invention. He went on a far-ranging lecture tour, telling the world his wonderful tale. The great discovery, he declared, had had its origin when he picked up a violin and fiddled a few notes. The notes set in motion harmonic vibrations, and he saw, in a flash of inspiration, how the vibrations of atoms could be used to create energy.

He set up the Keely Motor Company in New York and held a meeting at the plush Fifth Avenue Hotel. It was attended by bankers, businessmen, engineers, lawyers— a group of wealthy, adventurous individuals looking for a good investment. This was an era when great fortunes were being made in America by sharp-witted men. John D. Rockefeller was building his billion-dollar oil empire; Jay Gould, the Vanderbilts, E. H. Harriman, and others were earning millions from their railroad operations; and Andrew Carnegie was growing rich manufacturing steel. Miraculous inventions were just around the corner: Alexander Graham Bell and his telephone, Thomas Alva Edison and electric lights, phonographs, motion pictures. The Wright Brothers would soon be dreaming of airplanes. Other men would seek ways to build gasoline-powered "horseless carriages." And here was John Worrell Keely, offering a fantastic new source of power!

The investors flocked to his side. The day after his first meeting at the Fifth Avenue Hotel, Keely was given ten thousand dollars to continue his research, with the assurance that more funds would be forthcoming as he needed them.

He had awed his audience with phrases like "quadruple negative harmonics," "etheric disintegration," and "atomic triplets." He explained that his machine was a "hydro-pneumatic, pulsating vacuum engine," which was hooked up to a device he called a "liberator." The "liberator" was a series of highly sensitive tuning forks, whose vibrations disintegrated air and water, liberating "etheric force" of great power.

Keely demonstrated a model of his vacuum engine. He poured a glass of water into its intake, and moments later the engine rumbled to life. A gauge attached to it

75

showed that a pressure of fifty thousand pounds per square inch had been created. The audience gasped as etheric force ripped thick cables apart, bent iron bars, and fired bullets through foot-deep planks. The whole thing seemed incredible.

Speaking glibly and rapidly, Keely reeled off the wonders of his invention:

"With these three agents alone [air, water, and machine], unaided by any and every compound, heat electricity and galvanic action, I have produced in an unappreciable time by a simple manipulation of the machine, a vaporic substance at one expulsion of a volume of ten gallons having an elastic energy of 10,000 pounds to the square inch. . . . It has a vapor of so fine an order it will penetrate metal. . . . It is lighter than hydrogen and more powerful than steam or any explosives known. . . . I once drove an engine 800 revolutions a minute of forty horsepower with less than a thimbleful of water and kept it running fifteen days with the same water."

This, obviously, was not the same old perpetual motion that all intelligent people knew was an impossibility. Keely was not depending on such hopeless methods as weighted wheels or endlessly cycling water. A man had only to look in the *Encyclopaedia Britannica* to find out why those devices could not work. No, Keely had something brand new—etheric force. The stockholders of the Keely Motor Company smiled knowingly at one another, quietly congratulating themselves for their perception and farsightedness. They all knew that John W. Keely was going to make them millionaires.

With his financial backing assured, Keely set up a laboratory at 1420 North Twentieth Street in Philadelphia, and this became the headquarters of the Keely Motor Company. Money poured in, and he began to build full-scale machines. Within two years, on November 10, 1874, Keely was showing off to a proud group of stockholders his first "vibratory generator." This was a preliminary model for an even more ambitious machine, on which he would spend the next fourteen years. A newspaperman who attended the 1874 demonstration of the wonderful machine wrote that the generator operated "out of a bath tub from which a stream of water, passing through a goose-quill, sets the entire contrivance in motion."

The years went by. Keely toiled on. The Keely Motor Company showed no profits and paid no dividends, but Keely explained that he was still deep in research and development. One day soon, he said, the patience of the stockholders would be rewarded by a golden flow of cash.

Some of the stockholders were restless. By now, Bell's telephone was in public use, Edison had produced wonder after profitable wonder, and the first sputtering automobiles were chugging down highways at a hesitant pace. Meanwhile, their hero, Keely, had not yet put his motor into commercial use. The investors journeyed down to Philadelphia regularly. Keely received them graciously, showed them around the laboratory, demonstrated his machines. He invited them to watch him at work. "You won't disturb me," he assured them, as he became involved with humming generators and throbbing tuning forks.

From time to time, of course, Keely required new funds for "further research." The stockholders usually obliged. Keely would call a meeting of the board of directors, and generally would enhance his progress report by throwing in a few new technical terms each time. The old investors voted new funds; fresh capital came into the company too, from men anxious to get in on the eventual bonanza.

With the power from his motor, Keely declared, it would be possible to send a train of cars from Philadelphia to San Francisco with no fuel other than a single cup of water. A gallon of water would be enough to propel a steamship from New York to Liverpool and back again. (Actually, Keely was being conservative. We now know that if the energy contained in a gallon of water could be completely liberated, it could keep trains or ocean liners running for several years instead of just a few trips.)

One of Keely's most enthusiastic backers was a well-to-do widow named Mrs. Clara Jessup Bloomfield-Moore. Whenever the other stockholders fretted at the lack of results, Mrs. Bloomfield-Moore urged them to have faith in Keely. She invested heavily in the company herself, and encouraged her friends to do the same. Then, too,

78

she wrote glowing, high-flown articles about Keely that appeared in the most widely read magazines of the day. In one, she said that Keely's etheric force was "like the sun behind the clouds, the source of all light though itself unseen. It is the latent basis of all human knowledge. . . ."

As president of the Keely Motor Company, Keely found it necessary to live in high style at the stockholders' expense. It would not do, he told them, for the head of such an important enterprise to dress shabbily, to ride in broken-down carriages, or to live in a squalid house. They agreed. So a good deal of the investors' money went to support Keely in a manner he thought suitable for a company president. The rest was spent on ever more complex machinery.

His new prize was a "shifting resonator"—a forbidding-looking affair of wires, tubes, and adhesive plates, enclosed in a hollow brass sphere. This was linked by a series of wires to the famous motor itself, and to a transmitter that bristled with steel rods in such numbers that it looked like a mechanical porcupine. The resonator, Keely explained, carried seven different kinds of vibration, each "being capable of infinitesimal division." Keely would set the whole contraption going in a variety of ways: sometimes by playing a few notes on his violin, sometimes with a zither or a harmonica, sometimes by striking an ordinary tuning fork. Whatever the method, etheric force came forth, starting the motor. The motor itself was a sturdy iron hoop encircling a drum with eight spokes. When etheric force began to radiate, the big drum would begin to spin rapidly—dramatic testimony to the power of Keely's machine.

Keely declined to take out any patents on his masterpiece, however. Some of the stockholders were worried by this. Should he not protect their rights with a patent?

No, Keely said. A patent application would have to contain the essential information about the workings of his invention. But the invention, though it obviously worked, was not quite ready for commercial development. Keely told the investors that he feared some unscrupulous pirate might study his patent application, steal his basic ideas, adapt them in some slightly different form, and beat the Keely Motor Company to the market. It was far better, he insisted, to keep every detail of the project a secret until the grand moment arrived when etheric force could be put to moneymaking use. Otherwise, there was a good chance that the investment of the stockholders, and Keely's long years of toil, would all go for nothing.

By this time, many leading scientists and engineers had heard about Keely's wonderful motor, and they wanted to know how it worked. Was there such a thing as etheric force? Did Keely's vibrators really tap the energy of the atoms? Perhaps—but Keely's refusal to explain his methods was suspicious. Other engineers began to wonder about the possibility of a hoax. Was there some way of duplicating Keely's results through known techniques?

Yes, said the magazine *Scientific American*. In 1884, it ran an article describing a series of experiments aimed at discrediting Keely. Everything that Keely had done, the magazine said, could be duplicated using compressed air as the source of energy. Did Keely have a hidden compressed-air supply somewhere near his motor?

Keely sidestepped the attacks. The other engineers, he told his backers, were petty, envious, disappointed men. Unable to meet his enigmatic challenge, they were reduced to trying to pull him down to their level. He reminded them how scoffers had laughed at the inventors of the steamship, the telegraph, and the telephone. Every startling new advance, Keely said, was accompanied by this sort of sniping by prejudiced, ignorant men.

The hubbub died down. Keely went on experimenting, his secret undivulged. Mrs. Bloomfield-Moore, though her loyalty to Keely remained unshaken, came to him with a suggestion. Perhaps, she said, Keely ought to take Thomas Edison in as a partner and confide the secret in him. Edison was the world's most famous inventor; nobody dared to sneer at him any more. If Edison lent his great prestige to the Keely Motor Company, it would mean an end to the attacks on Keely himself.

Keely may have seen that it would be good public relations to make use of Edison's name, but he refused to hear of the idea. He would tell his secret to no one, certainly not to Edison. He had no need for another man's prestige, he insisted. Those who attacked him to-

81

day would praise him wildly tomorrow. And he went on asking the stockholders for money and building ever more grandiose machines.

He printed up a mysterious chart, as occult as anything ever drawn by a medieval astrologer, and handed it out to his long-suffering investors. It showed overlapping circles, cones of radiating lines, various oddly shaped figures, and a series of musical notations. Supposedly, the secret of the etheric vibrations was contained on the chart, and many of the stockholders framed their copies and displayed them with great satisfaction. What did it all mean? No one knew. But it looked very profound, terribly significant.

By 1898, Keely had kept his company running for twenty-six years without ever once putting a product on the market. It had not earned a penny in all that time. An army of investors had thrown hundreds of thousands of dollars into the Keely Motor Company, enabling its president and founder to live a comfortable and luxurious life while building his vibrators and liberators and generators. From year to year, he performed a delicate juggling act with the stockholders, persuading them that prosperity was just around the corner. And they believed him, for who could fail to be awed by the demonstrations he gave, by his glib talk, by his air of self-confidence?

Then, in 1898, Keely died. And his secret had died with him, the horrified investors found out. Nowhere had he set down any clue to the workings of his motor.

Mrs. Bloomfield-Moore, his most ardent supporter, followed him to the grave soon afterward. Upon her death, her son, Clarence B. Moore, rented the building that had housed Keely's laboratory. Clarence Moore had been forced to stand by helplessly for years while his mother showered Keely with cash; now he wanted to see just what the fast-talking inventor had been up to.

Moore got together an investigating group consisting of a well-known electrical engineer and two professors from the University of Pennsylvania. They prowled through Keely's building. The liberators and generators and other apparatus had been carried away by Keely's supporters. But one clue of the mystery still remained.

They found a big steel globe, weighing three tons, hidden in the cellar. It had an opening on its upper surface. Pipes and tubes lay nearby. It looked very much like some sort of compressed-air device—just as the *Scientific American* article had guessed, back in 1884!

Moore and his associates ripped up the flooring of the room in which Keely had conducted his demonstrations. Brass tubes ran downward through the floor, through cunningly designed holes in the walls, to the cellar— leading to the giant steel globe. The secret was out. Keely's motor had been powered by gusts of compressed air, rising from the globe in the cellar. Perhaps he had controlled the apparatus by using a foot-operated pedal in the floor, they guessed. When he picked up his violin or harmonica to create the "harmonic vibrations" that supposedly triggered the motor, he might well have 83 tapped on the pedal, as though beating time with his foot.

For a quarter of a century, Keely's financial backers had solemnly swallowed his brand of hokum. They did not change their minds now. They refused to accept Clarence Moore's exposé. Moore was "embittered," they declared, because his mother had invested heavily in Keely's company against his own wishes. He had deliberately set out to smear the dead Keely by way of proving his mother's folly. Some of Keely's supporters went on insisting, to the end of their days, that if Keely had lived only a few more years he would have brought about a new industrial revolution.

No one talks of etheric force today, and we have more effective ways of getting energy out of atoms. But the strange thing about John Worrell Keely is that he had an undeniable knack for gadgetry. If he had so chosen, he might perhaps have made a real contribution to technology employing compressed air—which eventually came to have considerable industrial use. His years of research might have produced something of true benefit.

Instead, he hoodwinked a group of foolish, money-hungry investors for a quarter of a century while doing nothing but constructing clever but useless machines. The investors probably got no more than they deserved. And Keely, who might have been another Edison, attained high rank in America's gallery of rogues.

6: *The Kensington Stone*

In November, 1898, a Swedish-
born farmer named Olof Ohman was hard at work clearing the land of his farm, in the township of Solem, Minnesota, not far from the village of Kensington. Ohman,
born in 1859, had come to the United States in 1881,
one of the many Swedish immigrants who settled in Minnesota. By saving his skimpy wages—at best laborers
got paid a dollar a day—Ohman was able to make the
first down payment on a tract of farmland in 1891. Now,
seven years later, he was still busy clearing off the trees. 85

He was a big, powerful man. His usual method of uprooting a tree was to dig a trench around it, cut the roots, and rock the trunk back and forth until he could pull the tree from the ground, roots and all. On this particular November day he set to work on an aspen tree whose trunk was ten inches in diameter at the base. When he yanked the tree from the ground, he was startled to find a flat stone, almost three feet long, clutched in the tree's roots. As he described it in an affidavit sworn a decade later, "The stone lay just beneath the surface of the ground in a slightly slanting position, with one corner almost protruding. The two largest roots of the tree clasped the stone in such a manner that the stone must have been there at least as long as the tree. One of the roots penetrated directly downward and was flat on the side next to the stone. The other root extended almost horizontally across the stone and made at its edge a right angled turn downward. At this turn the root was flattened on the side toward the stone."

Ohman paused to examine the strange stone. Brushing aside some of the dirt on its surface, he saw that it bore some sort of inscription. Puzzled, Ohman called his neighbor from the next farm, Nils Flaten, to take a look. Neither he nor Flaten could make much out of the inscription.

A few weeks later, Ohman showed the stone to J. P. Hedberg, who ran a real estate and insurance agency in Kensington. Like nearly everybody else in that part of the state, Hedberg was a native of Sweden. Ohman—

who could sign his name but not otherwise write—asked his countryman to help him discover the meaning of the inscription.

On January 1, 1899, Hedberg wrote a letter to Swan J. Turnblad, the editor of a Swedish-language paper published in Minneapolis. Even though both Hedberg and Turnblad were Swedes, Hedberg wrote his letter in English—of sorts. This is what he said:

"I enclose you a copy of an inscription on a stone found about 2 miles from Kensington by a O. Ohman he found it under a tree when Grubbing. he wanted I should go out and look at it and I told him to haul it in when he came (not thinking much of it) and he did so, and this is an exsest Copy of it the first part is of the flat side of the stone the other was on the flat edge. I thought I would send it to you as you perhaps have means to find out what it is—it appears to be old Greek letters. please let me hear from you and oblige."

The copy Hedberg enclosed showed an inscription of 219 characters. Three of them were in the Roman alphabet—the letters AVM, later interpreted as the initials of *"Ave Virgo Maria,"* or "Hail, Virgin Mary." Some of the other characters looked, as Hedberg had said, like ancient Greek or Phoenician letters of a kind that were sometimes reproduced in nineteenth-century books on the Bible.

The rest of the characters appeared to be Scandinavian runes. Runes are alphabetic characters that were used in Scandinavia and elsewhere in northern Europe 87 for about a thousand years. Perhaps derived from the earlier Greek alphabet, the runic letters first came into use about A.D. 400, but reached their widest spread in the eighth through eleventh centuries, when roving Vikings were ranging across the seas. When Christianity reached the northern countries about the year 1050, the Roman alphabet, the one we use today, came with it, and runic writing, as a relic of paganism, became obsolete. A few literary men continued to write in runes for several centuries thereafter. By the fourteenth century, runic writing was all but unknown in Scandinavia except in the runic calendar, a chart of holy days that remained in use. Since 1500 or so, runic writing has been the exclusive province of scholars.

What was a runic inscription doing tangled in the roots of a Minnesota tree? Until 1867, when the first white settlers arrived, the area around Kensington had been Indian territory. It would not have been very much more surprising to find an inscription in Egyptian hieroglyphics there.

Ohman stored his puzzling stone in a bank vault in Kensington for a while. The manager of the bank, recognizing the inscription as runic, sent a penciled copy of it to Professor O. J. Breda, head of the Department of Scandinavian Languages at the University of Minnesota. The Norwegian-born Professor Breda, though no expert on runes, knew something about them, and was able to work out a shaky translation of the inscription.

88   He could make out the word *Vinland*. That widened

his eyes in surprise. Vinland was the name of Leif Erikson's settlement in America, according to the old Norse saga that told of the Viking discovery of America in about the year 1000. Many reputable scholars accepted the Erikson story as authentic, agreeing that Vikings had landed in the Western Hemisphere five hundred years before Columbus. Did this inscription have anything to do with Leif Erikson's Vinland, Breda wondered? He translated as much of the stone as he could, leaving blanks for the words that defeated him. This is what he got:

"— Swedes and — Norwegians on a discovery journey from Vinland westward. We had camp — — — one day's journey north from this stone. We were out fishing one day. When we came home we found — men red with blood and dead. A.V.M. save us from evil. We have — men by the sea to look after our ships — days' journey from this island. Year —"

Breda decided that the inscription had to be a forgery. It spoke of Vinland, which had been occupied for only a few years after 1000, but the runes themselves were in a much later style characteristic of the thirteenth or fourteenth century. And there were other odd things about the inscription that led him to think that it must have been carved by some latter-day Swede with a knowledge of the old runic writing.

When Breda's translation was published by Turnblad's paper in February, 1899, however, it stirred great excitement among the Scandinavian settlers of Minnesota. They shrugged off the professor's opinion that the stone was a fake. Here, at last, was real proof of the Viking landings in America, they declared! Not only had Leif Erikson and his men actually reached the New World, but they had traveled as far inland as Minnesota! It was exciting, satisfying, dizzying news.

Meanwhile the stone itself was sent to Professor George O. Curme of Northwestern University, in Evanston, Illinois. Professor Curme, an authority on early Scandinavian languages, had heard about the stone and, on the basis of Breda's translation, had thought it might be genuine. A look at the actual stone changed his mind. The letters were carved in clear, sharp outlines, and they were lighter than the main face of the stone. Would they still seem so sharp after hundreds of years of exposure to Minnesota weather? Dr. Curme did not think so. The appearance of the stone argued that the inscription had been carved fairly recently. He called the stone "a clumsy fraud."

Photographs of the inscription went to the University of Oslo, Norway. Three runologists studied them and offered their opinion in April, 1899. They agreed with Professor Curme. The stone was a forgery, and a crude one at that. It had probably been carved, they said, by some Swede with a vague knowledge of runes. But it was full of errors and letters that no runologist had ever seen before.

90   All Kensington was plunged into gloom when the ca-

ble from Oslo arrived. If the professors all agreed that the stone was a fake, it must be so, the people agreed. But who had committed the fraud, then?

People began looking suspiciously at Olof Ohman. He was the one who had found the stone. Could he have carved it himself, and pretended to have unearthed it from the roots of a tree? Well, Ohman was not an educated man. He could scarcely read or write modern languages, let alone runes. Had one of his friends conspired with him to concoct the hoax? No one knew. But Ohman was probably involved in some way, it was whispered.

Angry and embarrassed, Ohman took the troublesome stone home and dumped it face down in front of his granary door. He used it as an anvil for hammering leather and for straightening bent nails, and every time he went into the granary he trod across the offending stone that had brought him so much shame. Kensington began to forget the whole awkward business of the fraudulent stone. Eight years went by, and the Kensington Stone remained in the realm of hoaxdom.

Then, in 1907, the whole issue was revived. A newcomer happened on the scene, heard about the ill-famed stone, and came to the conclusion that it was genuine. For more than fifty years and in many millions of words of print he crusaded on behalf of the Kensington Stone, maintaining almost single-handedly that it was not a hoax at all.

His name was Hjalmar R. Holand, a native of Norway, who had settled in the neighboring state of Wisconsin. Holand did not figure in the original controversy over the stone; in 1899 he was a student at the University of Wisconsin, doing research on early Scandinavian poetry. In 1907, though, the thirty-five-year-old Holand was preparing a book on the history of the Norwegian settlements in America. The course of his research took him through Wisconsin and Minnesota, and he came, ultimately, to the small village of Kensington. Someone there told him about Olof Ohman and his inscribed stone. Holand went out to nearby Solem to visit Ohman.

Ohman still felt a little touchy about the stone, but he showed it to Holand, explaining that certain professors in Norway and elsewhere had branded it a fraud. Holand examined the 230-pound stone, which was 31 inches long, 16 inches wide, and 6 inches thick. Part of the inscription, he saw, was on the face of the stone, and the rest on the 6-inch edge. Holand did not then see any reason to doubt the verdict of the experts, but he thought the stone looked attractive and interesting, and he asked Ohman if he cared to part with it. The farmer made Holand a present of the stone.

A few months later, Holand translated it. He was able to fill in the blanks in Breda's 1899 translation. In January, 1908, Holand published his version. (The words in parentheses are not in the inscription, but were added by Holand to make the text read more smoothly in English.) Holand's 1908 translation went as follows:

92

"(We are) 8 Goths [Swedes] and 22 Norwegians on (an) exploration journey from Vinland round about the west. We had camp by (a lake with) 2 skerries [rocky islets] one day's journey north from this stone. We were (out) and fished one day. After we came home (we) found ten of our men red with blood and dead. A.V.M. (Ave Virgo Maria) save (us) from evil."

He translated the lines on the edge of the stone this way:

"(We) have ten men by the sea to look after our ships fourteen days' journey from this island. (In the) year (of our Lord) 1362."

Holand's translation disposed of one of Professor Breda's important objections. If the stone really had been carved in 1362, it explained why the runes were in the fourteenth-century style and not in the style of the time of Leif Erikson. But the old sagas of the Viking visits to America said nothing about Vikings living there in 1362. The Vinland colony had been abandoned hundreds of years before. So the question still remained: What had Vikings been doing in Minnesota in 1362 or —for that matter—at any other time? Was it possible that they could have ventured so far inland, these rovers of the sea who had never been famous for overland exploration?

Yes, Holand said. He proceeded to pour forth a stream of articles defending the genuineness of the Ken-   93 sington Stone. He dragged poor Olof Ohman and his neighbor Nils Flaten to a notary public in 1909 to swear an affidavit describing the discovery of the stone. He challenged all the philologists and linguists of Europe and America to prove that the stone was false, and he turned to the Minnesota Historical Society, a group of amateur scholars, to have the stone verified.

The Minnesota Historical Society was very cooperative. It appointed a committee to examine the stone. Since no one on the committee knew anything about runes, they turned to someone who did—Hjalmar R. Holand, the owner and chief promoter of the stone. Was the inscription genuine, they asked him? Yes, he told them. And so the sixty-six-page report of the committee, issued in April, 1910, endorsed the Kensington Stone as an authentic relic of a Scandinavian expedition to Minnesota in 1362.

There were some other supporters, such as a Wisconsin State University professor named Hotchkiss, who said in 1909 that "I am persuaded that the inscription cannot have been made in recent years." But most of the experts remained skeptical. From the universities of Denmark, Norway, and Sweden there came practically unanimous condemnation. Professor George T. Flom of the University of Illinois studied the runes of the inscription and doubted their authenticity. Professor Chester N. Gould of the University of Illinois suggested that the perpetrator of the hoax had probably used a modern Scandinavian textbook of runic writing as his guide, adding extra characters as his imagination dictated. Authority after authority lined up against the stone.

Hjalmar R. Holand stood alone, defying the scholarly world. He had not discovered the stone, and he could not in any way be linked to a hoax charge involving it. He defended the stone as vehemently as if he had been accused of carving it himself. Over the years, he wrote countless magazine articles and at least four books. First came *The Kensington Stone,* which he published at his own expense in 1932. It was followed by *Westward from Vinland* in 1942 and *America 1355–1364* in 1946. The most recent was *Explorations in America Before Columbus* (1956).

Holand had his ups and downs in his defense of the Kensington Stone. Every few years, some reputable authority declares that the stone really is genuine—and then some equally reputable man denounces it all over again as a fraud. Most of the experts are solidly convinced that the stone is the work of a hoaxer, but Holand did have his supporters. His grandest moment came in 1948, when the Smithsonian Institution decided that the stone was worthy of display at the National Museum in Washington, D.C. For some time prior to that, the stone had been exhibited at Alexandria, Minnesota. When it went off to the National Museum, Alexandria dedicated a Runestone Memorial Park, whose central feature was a gigantic replica of the stone weighing almost 50,000 pounds.

Dr. William Thalbitzer was the controversial stone's

chief backer at the Smithsonian. In August, 1951, he published an essay declaring that the stone was genuine. Soon, though, the stone was back in Minnesota. Three Danish experts on runes published a report in 1951 that branded the Kensington Stone as a thorough-going forgery. They were so positive in their condemnation that the red-faced curators at the National Museum quickly hustled the stone out of Washington.

Almost sixty years of dispute have left a vast mountain of charges and countercharges. Is the stone a fake, or isn't it? Holand was so tireless in his defense that many people have been bowled over by his unending campaign. He was almost eighty-five years old when his fourth book on the Kensington Stone came out in 1956, and he showed no sign of fatigue then. Until he died in 1963, past the age of ninety, he continued to defend the stone. It's impossible not to admire that sort of persistence.

But what are the main arguments, pro and con, about the Kensington Stone?

First is the matter of the discovery itself, on that November day in 1898. Olof Ohman, who was accompanied only by his young son at the time, found the stone, or said he did, clutched in the roots of an aspen tree.

Holand claimed that the tree, with its ten-inch-thick base, must have been about seventy years old when Ohman dug it up. The first white settlers did not reach the area until 1867, when the tree had been growing some forty years. Presumably Indians did not carve the stone.

So *if* the tree were ten inches thick at the base, and *if* it were really seventy years old, then it could well have tangled its roots around a stone that had been lying on the ground since 1362.

But Ohman is the only man who saw the tree. In April, 1899, ten of Ohman's neighbors came out to view the hole in the ground where the tree had been. One of them, C. W. Van Dyke, later recalled that the group had guessed the age of the tree, from its remaining roots, at "about twelve years." Quite possibly, the stone could have been carved in the 1880's, covered by the tree, and found by Ohman in 1898. Or it may never have been entwined in the aspen's roots at all.

The fact that the stone's face does not show the effects of weathering has also aroused discussion. A Minnesota geologist named Winchell, who believed the stone was genuine, nevertheless was troubled by the weathering, or the lack thereof. He suggested that the stone must have lain underground and face down for five hundred years; otherwise, he said, the inscription's age could be no more than "fifteen or thirty years," and "probably less than thirty years."

One likewise wonders who put the stone there, if it really was carved in the fourteenth century. Certainly not visitors from Leif Erikson's Vinland, as even Holand admitted. The records of Viking visits to America in the eleventh century seem quite authentic to many people. Few important scholars seriously believe today that Christopher Columbus was the first European to land in the Western Hemisphere. But the same Norse sagas that tell us of Leif's visit to America tell us that the Vinland colony collapsed within a few years. The colonists quarreled bitterly, murdered one another, and suffered Indian attack. In 1121, the sagas and annals state, Bishop Eric Gnupsson sailed from Greenland to find out what had happened to the Vinland colony, and was never heard from again. The record of Norse visits to America ends there—almost 250 years before the alleged date of the Kensington Stone inscription.

Holand had an explanation, however.

By dint of much digging in old Scandinavian archives, Holand found a record of an expedition supposedly sent out in 1354 by King Magnus of Norway. It seemed that King Magnus had raised funds for an expedition to Russia, through which he would forcibly convert the pagan Russians to Christianity. But fearful plague—the Black Death—broke out in Russia, making such an expedition too dangerous. King Magnus cast about for some other direction. He was brimming with religious zeal and had plenty of cash on hand.

Someone suggested that he look toward Greenland instead. There was a Norse colony on that remote subarctic island, but it had had little contact with the home country in recent years. King Magnus had heard that the settlers of Greenland were beginning to stray from the Christian faith. So he chose a certain Paul Knutson to lead an expedition to Greenland and save Christianity there. Holand found a letter from King Magnus to Knutson which declared, "We ask that you accept this our command with a right good will for the cause [Christianity], inasmuch as we do it for the honor of God and for our predecessors, who in Greenland established Christianity and have maintained it until this time, and we will not let it perish in our days. Know this for truth, that whoever defies this our command will meet with our serious displeasure and receive full punishment."

That letter, which was dated 1354, no longer exists. It was destroyed during a fire that ravaged Copenhagen in 1728. What Holand found was a copy, made in the sixteenth century, that survived the fire.

There is no reason to doubt that the letter is genuine. Very likely Paul Knutson did lead an expedition to Greenland in the middle of the fourteenth century, or at least was commanded to do so. But what is very much open to question is the fanciful theory that Hjalmar Holand built out of this single scrap of paper.

Holand thought that Knutson reached Greenland and found that many of the colonists had emigrated to Vinland, that is, to America. Vinland was supposedly only a few days' sailing to the southwest of Greenland. So, Holand argued, Knutson obeyed the orders of his king, who had told him to contact the Greenlanders, and followed them to Vinland.

And then? Vinland was on the Atlantic coast. Holand suggested that Knutson's party failed to find the settlement. The explorers spent years combing the shores of North America without success. Finally, they split up.   99

Ten men remained by the sea to look after the ships. The rest set out on a fantastic journey inland, evidently to look for the vanished settlers.

Holand thought that the Norsemen entered Hudson Bay, found the mouth of the Nelson River, traveled down the Nelson on a southwesterly course into Lake Winnipeg, crossed the lake and discovered the mouth of the Red River, and followed that river southward for some three hundred miles. Then, he said, the roving Vikings turned eastward along the Buffalo River, reaching Lake Cormorant in Minnesota (the "lake with the two skerries" mentioned on the Kensington Stone) and then, by hauling their boat overland where necessary, by rowing, and by crossing rivers and small lakes, they reached the place that would one day be Olof Ohman's farm. There they were attacked by Indians, suffered heavy losses, carved a rune stone as a memorial for the dead and as a notice they had been there, and withdrew.

The Kensington Stone refers to its location as "this island." Olof Ohman's farmland was no island at all, but rather a slight rise in a rolling prairie. Holand found geological evidence that the prairie probably was flooded in the fourteenth century, which would have made the Ohman farm a true island. Since that would match the description on the stone, it must count as a point in Holand's favor. All the rest of his theory, though, seems like the wildest guesswork.

One immediate question is, did Paul Knutson ever leave Norway? Other records tell us that in 1355, the

year after the king's decree, the weather in the north
Atlantic was so bad that no ships could sail westward. In
that same year, King Magnus turned the crown of Norway over to his son, Prince Haakon. Under Haakon, the
man who had originally suggested the Greenland expedition—one Orm Östenson—fell from favor and was ex-
ecuted. So perhaps the expedition was canceled. Magnus
himself was also King of Sweden, but he had his hands
full there from 1356 on with a series of rebellions led by
another son, Prince Erik. So there are many reasons for
thinking that Paul Knutson stayed home.

If he did go to Greenland, what proof is there that he
continued on to North America? None. We have only
Holand's guess. There are no records of Knutson's voyage, none of his experiences in Greenland, none of his
return to Norway.

Holand's theory gets its hardest test if we assume that
Knutson did go from Greenland to Vinland, spent seven
years or so looking for the lost colonists, and made his
inland venture in 1362. The Kensington Stone declares
that the voyagers had come "fourteen days' journey"
from the sea, which means that in just two weeks they
traveled from Hudson Bay to Minnesota, over an unknown route. It hardly seems likely. As Erik Wahlgren,
professor of Scandinavian languages at the University
of California at Los Angeles and an unbeliever in the
stone, has written, "In more ways than one, this was the
most remarkable voyage in human history. In spite of
time out for fishing—as guaranteed by the inscription—   101

the Norsemen made the well-nigh impossible ascent of the Nelson, its 47 portages and all, followed by seemingly endless hundreds of miles of trackless lake, river, and swamp, some 2,000 miles by even the most economical, mapped-out route (and doubtless twice or thrice that as the strangers must have wandered) in the space of fourteen days!"

Holand himself came to see the absurdity of that. He offered instead a new but equally improbable explanation. He said that a "day's journey" had an artificial meaning to the Norsemen, that it was understood to be the "average distance covered in a day's sailing or rowing" and "was equal to about seventy-five English miles or a little more." Thus the term did not refer to actual days of travel, but was simply a unit of measure. The straight-line distance from the mouth of the Nelson River to Kensington is about eleven hundred miles, or roughly fourteen "day's journeys" by Holand's new system of computing, though he admitted that the real journey may have taken months. Such reasoning is a little strained, at best.

So is the theory of a Holand supporter named Charles Michael Boland, who has written a book designed to "prove" that not only Norsemen but also Phoenicians, Chinese, Romans, and Irishmen visited America before Columbus. Boland can't accept Holand's reasoning in this matter either. He thinks that the Norsemen reached Minnesota by marching inland a way, building a ship, 102 and sailing across Lake Superior. Lake Superior, he says, is the "sea" that Kensington is fourteen days' journey from.

Fine, except that the text of the stone uses the word *hawet*, which specifically means "*saltwater* sea." Lake Superior is large enough to seem like a sea, but its water is fresh. Were these Vikings unable to notice that?

The sharpest attack on the Kensington Stone has been directed against the language itself. Erik Wahlgren has declared that the language of the stone (not the alphabet in which it is written) is modern Swedish, with at least one Norwegian word thrown in, *opdagelse,* "exploration." Other critics have shown that the inscription even includes a few English words, as well as a good many runic letters that simply were unknown in the fourteenth century. Holand had explanations to answer these various charges. The controversy is extremely complicated, and, in fairness to Holand, it should be said that his replies to some of the attacks sound very reasonable to a layman. But most of the professors whose lifework it has been to study Scandinavian runes share Erik Wahlgren's opinion that "On no possible score, then, can the Minnesota rune stone be accepted as ancient. And if it is not ancient, it is modern and thus a hoax. . . ."

Which leaves us with the hardest problem of all: Who was the hoaxer?

In 1910, a small Norwegian weekly published in Wisconsin, *Amerika,* ran an article by its editor, Rasmus B. Anderson, about the Kensington Stone. Anderson had once been a professor at the University of Wisconsin. He   103 told how a Swede named Andrew Anderson, no relative of his, had visited him and had told him about the possible origin of the Kensington Stone.

According to Andrew Anderson, Ohman was not illiterate at all. "He is not a college-bred man, but has always been a great reader," with a fondness for works of science, history, and philosophy. Among Ohman's friends was one Sven Fogelblad, a former clergyman interested in such scholarly matters as runic writing. Fogelblad, so Andrew Anderson said, owned a book about runes. So did Ohman: a reference work called *The Well-Informed Schoolmaster*, which had pictures of the old runic alphabets.

Rasmus Anderson wrote, "The three, Fogelblad, Anderson, and Ohman frequently discussed the runes when they were together, Fogelblad writing long sentences in runic on paper and explaining them to Ohman. . . . All three were deeply interested in runes and either one of them was capable of producing the rune-stone in question."

Holand denied Rasmus Anderson's charges, point by point. He insisted that Ohman had no education and knew nothing about runes, that Andrew Anderson was no scholar either and not even a friend of Ohman's, and that Fogelblad was lazy, ignorant, and owned no books on runes. Ohman too, in a letter written in 1910, denied the entire Anderson story—though of course that proves nothing, if Ohman were in on the hoax. One point Holand did admit: that Ohman was not quite the slow-witted farmer he was said to be, for he owned a few books, including a Swedish grammar text and a copy of *The Well-Informed Schoolmaster,* and the latter book did indeed contain illustrations of the runic alphabet.

The Kensington Stone remains a mystery today. But for the ingenuity and energy of Hjalmar Holand, it would be an all-but-forgotten hoax. Holand managed to persuade a fair number of people, particularly in the region around Minnesota, that the stone is a genuine relic of a fourteenth-century Norse visit to North America's interior.

It would be pleasant to think so, and exciting to contemplate the bravery of those thirty Vikings who made such a great voyage of exploration. Cold scientific scrutiny, though, is often the enemy of romance. Despite Holand's decades-long campaign, the weight of evidence seems against him. The truth appears to be that the Kensington Stone was the work of a few clever Swedes in nineteenth-century Minnesota, with a knowledge of runes, a knack for stone-carving, and an urge to glorify the deeds of their ancestors. Perhaps Olof Ohman was in on the hoax, and perhaps he was innocent. Holand himself is certainly in the clear. He was no hoaxer, though he seems guilty of self-delusion.

Oddly, there is one slim possibility that the Kensington Stone may be genuine after all. In 1738, a French explorer, the Sieur de La Vérendrye, undertook an expedition west of Lake Superior. In what is now central North Dakota, he discovered a curious stone inscribed on both sides with mysterious characters. When he returned to Quebec in 1743, he brought the stone with him, and showed it to some Jesuit priests.

They could not decipher the inscription. Consulting their books, though, they found that the writing looked very much like "Tataric," the script of the Tatars of Central Asia. This seemed strange, and the stone was sent on to Paris for further study.

Does that mean that Tatars somehow traveled out of Mongolia into North America? Not really. But, according to the *Encyclopaedia Britannica*, early Tatar inscriptions "bear a superficial resemblance to runes," though this is just a coincidence and there is no connection with Scandinavia.

Could it be that the carvers of the Kensington Stone ventured even farther west and set up a second rune stone? And that the French Jesuits innocently and understandably mistook those runes for Tataric?

Very possibly. Holand tells us that "only an expert in runic or Tatarian writing would be able to distinguish between the two," and the priests at Quebec were neither. An examination of Vérendrye's stone, then, would explain a great deal. An expert on runes could translate its inscription, which would certainly be a genuine Norse relic, since nobody in North Dakota in 1738 knew anything about runes. Vérendrye's stone could not be a forgery, and therefore that other rune stone, the famous one from Minnesota, would probably be authentic too.

But where is the Vérendrye stone?

It was last heard of in eighteenth-century Paris. Holand went to Europe in 1911 to look for it, but no one had heard of it in any Parisian museum. He looked again in 1928 and in 1950, without luck. The stone has disappeared, and with it a good chance of proving that Norsemen visited the heart of North America before Columbus was born. So long as Vérendrye's find remains a phantom, the Kensington Stone must be considered a hoax.

7: *Dr. Cook and the North Pole*

As this century began, one of the most exciting events that claimed public attention was the race to reach the North Pole. The South Pole, off in remote, frigid Antarctica, did not seem to hold the same interest. But men vied with one another to get to "the top of the world," the place where the meridians met, latitude 90° North.

It was no easy task. The bitter cold was only one of the difficulties. There is no Arctic continent; the North Pole is an imaginary point in the middle of a frozen sea.

No one knew that as a certainty, of course, in the nineteenth century, but it seemed quite likely. Anyone seeking the Pole had to travel over a relatively thin crust of ice, which might break up or give way at any moment.

The earliest voyagers northward simply went as far as they could go by boat, turning back when the solidly frozen sea blocked further advance. In the sixteenth and seventeenth centuries, explorers of England and the Netherlands tried the Arctic adventure repeatedly, not for any scientific purpose but simply in the hope of finding a clear trade route to the Orient. Many lost their lives in the attempt to get through the ice.

Gradually, the quest became more scientific in nature. Men wanted to reach the North Pole for the sake of knowledge alone. In 1827, Sir Edward Parry of England led an expedition that pioneered a new method. He proposed to reach the Pole "by means of traveling with sledge-boats over the ice, or through any spaces of water that might occur." Where the sea was frozen, the men would drag the runner-equipped boats over the ice; where the ice was broken, they would row.

Parry's expedition met with dreadful difficulties— rain, melting ice, and endless discomfort. One day the ice opened and closed so often that four hours of unloading and reloading the boats were needed to advance half a mile. When they slogged forward over firm ice, they also met problems: the entire ice field was drifting southward even as they toiled toward the Pole. It was like a giant treadmill. While they rested each day, the 109 drift of the ice undid all that they had gained. Parry gave up, finally, at 82°45'N.—closer to the Pole than anyone had been before.

Other explorers followed. An English expedition led by Sir George Nares broke Parry's record in 1875, and then Americans under A. W. Greely surpassed Nares by four miles in 1882, getting to 83°24'N. Twelve years later, Fridtjof Nansen's Norwegian expedition got to 86°12'; Italians got twenty-two miles closer to the Pole in 1901. New expeditions were planned, each benefiting from the experiences of those who had gone before.

Why go to the North Pole, anyway?

The simplest reason was the one another man gave for climbing Mount Everest: "Because it is there." The Pole was the symbol of all questing, all the romance of exploration. It was the unattainable goal of every explorer's dreams.

There were also good scientific reasons for Arctic exploration. Much needed to be learned about the conditions of life in the far north, about the possibility of land at the Pole, about the geography of the Arctic regions. However, it was not necessary to get all the way to 90° N. to make these scientific observations. The same data could be gathered fifty miles short of the Pole, without loss. As one polar explorer put it, "the actual attainment [of the Pole] was of no scientific importance, but it was of value as an ultimate objective and the lure of the Pole led men onward into the unknown, and thus served science in its day."

110

The twentieth century opened with the Pole still unconquered, though it seemed certain that someone was bound to reach it before the new century was a decade old. And, in fact, the world learned in 1909 that the North Pole had been reached at last—by two separate and independent expeditions, both led by Americans.

No sooner was the news out than fierce controversy erupted. One of the explorers called the other a liar and a fraud. The other explorer answered back. The public debated. Had the suspected hoaxer reached the Pole or not? For that matter, had the other man really gotten there?

Nobody knew. Had the Pole been reached by one man, or two—or none?

The man who claimed to have been first at the North Pole was Dr. Frederick Albert Cook, a surgeon, anthropologist, and experienced explorer who had been both to the Arctic and to the Antarctic on earlier expeditions. Cook was born in 1865 in upstate New York, the youngest of four children. His parents were Germans who had come to the United States about 1850. The family name was originally Koch, changed to Cook in the year of Frederick's birth. Dr. Cook does not seem to have been related to "Dr." Albert Koch, the fabricator of sea serpents, whose reputation was very much like his own—shady.

Cook's father, a physician, died when the boy was five. As he entered his teens, Frederick supported himself by doing odd jobs, and managed to scrape together enough money to send himself to college at Columbia. He went on to spend a year at Columbia's medical school, the College of Physicians and Surgeons, and finished his medical education at New York University. He went into medical practice in 1890, but few patients visited the young doctor. Cook had always been fascinated by exploration and adventure, and with his practice so slow, he yearned to leave New York for some more exciting place.

The chance came early in 1891. A man whose name will always be linked with Cook's, Robert E. Peary, was outfitting an Arctic expedition, and he advertised for a surgeon. Cook answered the ad. Peary gave him the job.

Peary, eleven years older than Cook, was a single-minded, dedicated man, determined to be the first to reach the North Pole. He was not a likable person, though many admired him for his courage and energy. There was something cold and forbidding about Peary, as though the Arctic had touched his soul. He seemed to live only for the Pole. Science, music, the arts, literature —none of these things mattered to him. What drove him on was the urge to plant the American flag at 90° N.

He was a civil engineer attached to the United States Navy, and approached the polar project as an engineering challenge. Methodically and laboriously he studied the records of other Arctic expeditions, plotted possible routes, and above all worked to master the Eskimo techniques of travel in the far north. The Eskimos, after all,

112

were natives of the Arctic, and knew how to cope with the problems it presented. They had no interest in reaching the Pole, but Peary, using their methods, did.

As early as 1881 Peary had written in his diary about Columbus, "whose fame can be equalled," he said, "only by him who shall one day stand with 360 degrees of longitude beneath his motionless feet and for whom East and West shall have vanished—the discoverer of the North Pole." Peary first visited the Arctic five years later, journeying to Greenland to make a preliminary study of the polar region. By 1891, he had found enough supporters so that he could raise money for a full-scale expedition toward the Pole. The expedition sailed from Brooklyn on June 6, 1891. Cook was aboard as the party's surgeon. Also present, to universal astonishment, was Peary's wife—the first woman to be taken on a polar expedition.

Cook and Peary got along well. The expedition headed north across the Greenland Ice Cap, and, after 130 miles of hard travel, when some of the explorers were tired, Dr. Cook "was the first to volunteer to go on," Peary later wrote. Peary called Cook "always helpful and an indefatigable worker," and paid tribute to his "unruffled patience and coolness in an emergency." When Peary broke his leg in a shipboard accident, Cook treated him, and Peary later declared, "Thanks to the professional skill of my surgeon Dr. Cook, my complete recovery was rapidly attained."

The expedition did not get north of Greenland; Peary   113

was still preparing himself for the great attempt on the Pole. In 1893, Peary returned to the Arctic, once again with his wife, but with Cook not present. Cook had already committed himself to a three-month Arctic cruise aboard another ship.

Peary's 1893 expedition was notable chiefly because Mrs. Peary gave birth to a daughter in Greenland—the first baby ever born on an Arctic expedition. Cook's cruise took him to northern Greenland, where he continued the studies of Eskimo life that he had begun on his first Arctic trip, studies that Peary had called "most valuable. . . . A record of the tribe unapproachable in ethnological archives."

Cook returned to the Arctic in 1894 aboard the yacht *Miranda.* When the yacht struck an iceberg off southern Greenland, Cook distinguished himself by bravely traveling ninety miles through ice-strewn waters in a small open boat to summon a rescue ship. For the next three years, he practiced medicine in New York, while dreaming of polar adventure. Peary, meanwhile, continued to lay the plans for his next attempt to win the Pole.

In 1897, Cook had a new opportunity for exploration —at the opposite end of the earth. A Belgian expedition to the Antarctic had been organized, and, that August, Cook learned that its departure from Belgium had been delayed by the resignation of the ship's surgeon. Cook wired an offer to the expedition's leader, Adrien de Gerlache, to take the job. The Belgian knew of Cook's earlier Arctic experience, and accepted his offer, telling him to meet the ship in Rio de Janeiro at the end of September.

The *Belgica,* which Cook boarded at Rio, had a truly international crew, with Russians, Romanians, Belgians, and Norwegians aboard. Nearly everyone spoke some German, as did Cook, and so communication took place in that language. One member of the expedition was a twenty-five-year-old Norwegian named Roald Amundsen, just beginning a great career as an explorer. Some years hence, Amundsen would gain fame as the first man to cross from the Atlantic to the Pacific via the Northwest Passage, and then would crown that accomplishment in 1911 by winning the race to the South Pole.

Amundsen was impressed by Cook's behavior on the voyage of the *Belgica.* The expedition met with extraordinary difficulties; the ship was caught in the ice, and forced to spend thirteen months gripped by the pack. They were not prepared for a winter's stay in the Antarctic, and the men of the expedition suffered terribly in the long darkness. Scurvy plagued their bodies and mental depression affected their minds. Cook, as the ship's surgeon, was a tower of strength during this trying time. Amundsen wrote later that Cook, "of all the ship's company, was the one man of unfaltering courage, unfailing hope, endless cheerfulness, and unwearied kindness. When anyone was sick, he was at his bedside to comfort him; when anyone was disheartened, he was there to encourage. And not only was his faith undaunted, but his ingenuity and enterprise were boundless." According to

115

Amundsen, Cook was chiefly responsible for the survival of the *Belgica* party as it waited for the ice to release the ship. "He was beloved and respected by all . . . upright, capable, and conscientious in the extreme."

So far, there is nothing in Cook's record that would indicate he was capable of the most shameless hoax of the twentieth century. He had served with distinction on three Arctic and one Antarctic expeditions, and no one had anything but praise for his character and professional skill.

However, one incident on the *Belgica* cruise gave a hint of the notorious Cook of later years. As the expedition headed southward, it stopped in Tierra del Fuego, that lonely, windswept land at the tip of South America. A British missionary named Thomas Bridges had been living there for some years, studying the language and customs of the Yahgan Indians. Cook, an experienced anthropologist himself, struck up a friendship with Bridges, and discovered that the missionary had compiled a dictionary containing over thirty thousand words of the Yahgan language—a unique and irreplaceable document.

Cook offered to carry the manuscript back to the United States and arrange for its publication. Bridges did not wish to let Cook take the only existing copy of the dictionary with him to Antarctica, but he agreed to let him pick it up on his return voyage north. Bridges died the following year; in 1899, when the *Belgica* finally extricated itself from the ice pack, it called at

116

Tierra del Fuego, and Bridges' family, remembering the promise, turned the manuscript over to Cook.

Many years went by. Cook wrote a few letters to the Bridges family, speaking vaguely of "difficulties" in getting the work published. Then nothing more was heard. Lucas Bridges, the missionary's son, tried in vain to get the manuscript back.

Cook, meanwhile, was offering the lifework of Thomas Bridges as his own compilation. A New York *Times* article in 1901, commenting on the results of the *Belgica* expedition, remarked, "Besides medical and anthropological reports, Dr. Cook will make a notable contribution in the shape of an extensive vocabulary of the Yahgan language, the hitherto unknown speech of the savage inhabitants of Tierra del Fuego." Not a word was said about Bridges or his authorship of the monumental Yahgan dictionary.

Shortly before World War I, a group of Scandinavian scientists visited Tierra del Fuego. Lucas Bridges asked them about his father's dictionary, and learned that it was at last about to see print—to be published in Belgium, backed by a grant from the Belgian Parliament. And it was going to bear Cook's name!

Lucas Bridges hurried to Belgium. He saw an advance proof of the dictionary's cover, which credited the work to "Frederick A. Cook, Dr. of Anthropology." (Cook was a doctor of medicine, with no formal degrees in anthropology.) In small print at the bottom of the page was a line mentioning the Reverend Thomas Bridges, 117 who had been "instrumental in collecting the words."

When they learned the truth, the Belgian publishers agreed to give Thomas Bridges his proper credit, listing Cook only as someone who had aided in bringing the work to publication. But World War I broke out before the dictionary could be published. Belgium was brutally invaded by Germany, and the precious manuscript vanished in the confusion.

It did not turn up again until 1929—in Germany. A daughter of Thomas Bridges learned it had been found, journeyed to Europe, and arranged for the book's publication, which eventually took place in 1933. Cook's chicanery had kept it from the world for a third of a century.

Cook's reputation was still untarnished in 1900. His book about the *Belgica* expedition, *Through the First Antarctic Night*, was widely read, and acclaimed as a valuable document on the psychological effects of spending a winter in Antarctic darkness. His medical practice flourished. He was one of America's best-known explorers.

Peary still was hammering away at the Arctic. In 1899, he had gotten as far north as 85°51', though the attempt saw him lose eight toes to frostbite. Undaunted, he explored northern Greenland in 1900, and made another polar thrust in 1901. For months, Peary, his wife, and his infant daughter were out of contact with the rest of the world, and many of Peary's friends feared that he had been lost. An expedition was organized to search for them, and Cook was aboard the relief ship, the *Erik*, when it sailed from Nova Scotia in 1901.

Peary, who had not been lost at all, was found—safe, but in poor health. Cook recommended that he go home for a rest. Peary refused. He had one year remaining of a five-year leave of absence from the Navy, and he intended to make the most of it. He plunged north again, getting only to 84° 17′. By August, 1902, Peary was back in the United States, already planning the next expedition, which would be his seventh.

Cook's attention turned next to mountain climbing. Though he was a short, slender man, his physical endurance seemed boundless, and in 1903 he set out to climb Alaska's Mount McKinley, the highest peak in North America. The attempt failed. In 1906, Cook tried again.

Peary was once more in the Arctic while Cook was scaling McKinley the second time. He had left in July, 1905, and the following spring had sledged across the frozen Arctic Ocean to latitude 87°6′N., just 174 miles from the Pole. No man had ever been closer. There, exhaustion, dwindling supplies, and frequent open water had turned Peary back. It was an incredible exploit for a man of fifty, but Peary, driven on by his obsession with the North Pole, was not satisfied. He could not rest until he had reached 90°N.

Cook had had better luck with his expedition—so he said. He made his climb late in the summer of 1906. His party met with difficulties, and in August most of the

119

members of the expedition decided the attempt was hopeless. They withdrew, but Cook, accompanied only by a man named Edward Barrille, gave it one more try. On September 27, 1906, Cook wired from Alaska the news that he and Barrille had reached the summit of the hitherto unclimbed mountain by a route up a northeast ridge. He talked of the "ridiculous ease" with which he had climbed from a camp at 16,300 feet to the highest peak at "20,391 feet." (Mount McKinley is actually 20,270 feet at its highest point.)

Experienced mountain climbers, including the other members of Cook's own expedition, were startled and skeptical. They did not see how Cook could possibly have made the ascent in the short time he claimed, particularly so late in the year, when the weather would be against him. But Cook published a book, *To the Top of the Continent*, telling the story of his exploit and including photographs that he said showed the summit of the mountain. As a result he was in great demand as a lecturer and traveled around the country as the "Conqueror of McKinley," describing his feat.

No one publicly called Cook a liar, but there was a great deal of private whispering. Gossip out of Alaska had it that Cook had never been near the summit, but had bribed Barrille, a man of no great reputation, to back up his story. Barrille, so it was murmured, had told a few of his friends that Cook's claim was a fake.

One of those who heard the anti-Cook gossip was the Arctic explorer Vilhjalmur Stefansson, a friend of

Peary's. Stefansson visited Alaska in 1907, heard the stories, and warned Peary that Cook, having faked a climb of Mount McKinley, might now go on to fake a trip to the North Pole.

Peary, who was then planning his own new polar expedition, brushed the suggestion aside. "Cook is an honorable man," Peary told Stefansson, who later wrote that "Peary made me feel like a worm" for suggesting such a thing.

Not until 1909, when Cook claimed to have reached the North Pole, did anyone openly challenge his Mount McKinley exploit. A week after Cook's new claim, one member of his 1906 expedition said, "I am just as sure as that I am living that Cook never saw the North Pole. Any man who made the representations he did of his alleged ascent of Mount McKinley is capable of making the statements credited to him in the press today." Barrille, too, spoke up, confessing that Cook had promised him money for keeping quiet about the fraud. He had never said so before, he declared, because he had failed to collect from Cook, and had been hoping eventually to get his money.

Cook answered these charges by saying that Barrille had been bribed by his enemies to call him a liar. Barrille then told Cook to his face that they had never been to the top of Mount McKinley. Cook threatened to sue for libel, but never did.

The question was settled in 1913, when Hudson Stuck, a mountain-climbing clergyman, climbed McKinley and   121 declared, "The claims that Doctor Cook made on his return are well known, but it is quite impossible to follow his course from the description given in his book." Nor did Cook's photos of the summit resemble in any way what Stuck saw when he got there. Another climber, Belmore Browne, published a photograph of a mountain he called "Fake Peak," twenty miles from McKinley's summit and only 8,000 feet high. The photograph matched Cook's photos of "McKinley's summit." In 1955 and 1956, Bradford Washburn, director of the Boston Museum of Science and himself a three-time climber of Mount McKinley, made a detailed study of the area and showed convincingly that Cook had indeed tried to pass off photographs of a lesser peak as those of McKinley's summit.

He had stolen another man's dictionary, and he had lied about his conquest of Mount McKinley. But the public knew nothing about any of this in 1907. They knew Cook only as a bold and valiant explorer of whom the United States could be proud. Cook now talked of attaining the North Pole, and few doubted that he would— possibly even grasping the great prize away from Robert Peary, who had sought it so stubbornly for half his life.

With the backing of President Theodore Roosevelt and many wealthy Americans, Peary was then organizing the most ambitious of all his polar expeditions. He planned to set out in the summer of 1907, but his ship, the *Roosevelt,* was not ready on time, and it was necessary to wait until the following July. Peary, fifty-two

122

years old, was keenly disappointed at the delay, for age was beginning to slow him down. He did not then know what grief that year's delay was destined to cause him.

Cook was on the way. Early in 1907, he had lunched with a millionaire friend, John R. Bradley. Bradley invited Cook to go north with him on a hunting trip. Cook suggested, instead, that they go to the North Pole.

"Not I," said Bradley. "Would you like to try for it?"

"There's nothing that I would rather do," Cook replied. "It's the ambition of my life."

Bradley agreed to finance an expedition. The planning was done quietly, with none of the publicity and fanfare that Peary's expedition was getting. Cook's plan was to spend the winter of 1907–08 in Greenland, setting out across the ice for the Pole after gathering supplies and hiring Eskimos. On July 3, 1907, Bradley and Cook set out from Gloucester, Massachusetts, aboard the yacht *John R. Bradley;* so far as anyone else knew, it was merely a hunting expedition.

On August 27, the yacht landed at Annoatok, Greenland—just fifteen miles north of Etah, which Peary intended to use as a base on his expedition. The Eskimos, expecting Peary in 1907, had trained sledge dogs and assembled a large store of provisions. Cook was able to hire some of these men and their dogs and to buy supplies of walrus skin and fat from them.

The *Bradley* dropped Cook and one companion, Rudolph Francke, off at Annoatok and returned to the   123

United States. Bradley brought back a letter from Cook, announcing publicly his intention of going to the Pole.

Peary's friends were aghast. Could it be that another man, using Peary's methods and even his Eskimos, would rob Peary of the triumph that should be his? Peary himself, fretting out his postponement, doubted that Cook would succeed, but did not like the idea that Cook was hiring away his men and buying the provisions that had been collected for him. Those were actions, Peary said, "of which no man possessing a sense of honor would be guilty."

Cook and Francke, unaware of the storm of disapproval they had raised, left Annoatok at eight in the morning on February 19, 1908, with 11 sledges, 10 Eskimos, and 103 Arctic huskies. Cook carried a ton of food to be used while crossing Greenland and two tons more for the trip across the polar sea. Four days later, he sent Francke back to guard the depot at Annoatok, and continued on alone.

His plan was to cross Smith Sound to Ellesmere Island, and then to continue over to Axel Heiberg Island, follow it to its northern tip at Cape Thomas Hubbard, and set out over the frozen sea for the Pole, some five hundred miles farther north. Just what Cook actually did during the fourteen months he was away from civilization is, of course, a mystery that will never be solved. But this is what he claimed to have done.

Though hampered by temperatures as low as 83° F.
124   below zero, Cook reached Cape Thomas Hubbard by the

middle of March. His Eskimos built igloos there, and the party rested a few days. On March 18, Cook selected two young Eskimos to go with him to the Pole: Etukishook and Ahwelah. Two others would accompany them part of the way. The rest would go back to Annoatok.

Cook set out on the eighteenth with two sledges, pulled by twenty-six dogs. He carried what he calculated was an eighty-day supply of food, allowing one pound of pemmican (dried meat) a day. He planned to use twenty of his dogs for food on the homeward trip, a common practice among polar explorers.

Northward they went, making twenty-six miles the first day, twenty-one the second, and sixteen the third. Axel Heiberg Island dropped far behind. The shapes of snow peaks seemed to Cook like "huge creatures, mis-shapen and grotesque." The temperature reached 59° F. below zero. "Our moistened lashes quickly froze together as we winked, and when we rubbed them and drew apart the lids the icicles broke the tender skin."

On March 22, Cook came to open water and camped, still four hundred miles from the Pole. During the night thin ice formed, and the three men hurried across to the firmer ice beyond. A gale rose, and they huddled for warmth in a hastily constructed igloo. While they waited out the storm, the ice cracked beneath the igloo. Cook was dumped into the sea, but his Eskimos quickly pulled him out. The storm died down; they proceeded north-ward. On March 26, Cook figured his position at 84° 24'N.

Four days later, Cook sighted land to the west. "I felt a thrill such as Columbus must have felt when the first green vision of America loomed before his eye," he wrote. Barren, ice-shielded land lay parallel to his line of march for some fifty miles. He named it Bradley Land, after his backer.

Now the journey became monotonous, a matter of day-by-day sledging. On April 14, he was only a hundred miles from the Pole; five days later, at 89°31′N., less than thirty miles separated him from his goal. He told his Eskimos that they would soon be at "the big nail" —their term for the top of the world.

Midnight of April 20–21 passed, as they got beyond 89°46′. "Cracking our whips, we bounded ahead," Cook wrote. "The boys sang. The dogs howled. . . . Constantly and carefully I watched my instruments in recording this final reach. Nearer and nearer they recorded our approach. We were all lifted to the paradise of winners as we stepped over the snows of a destiny for which we had risked life and willingly suffered the tortures of an icy hell. . . . Step by step my heart filled with a strange rapture of conquest . . . we touched the mark . . . there is sunrise within us. . . . We are at the top of the world!"

Cook did not find the North Pole attractive. "What a cheerless spot to have aroused the ambition of man for so many ages!" he declared. "No life. No land. No spot to relieve the monotony of frost. We were the only pulsating creatures in a dead world of ice."

126

It was April 21, 1908. "With a step, it was possible to go from one part of the globe to the opposite side. . . . North, east, and west had vanished. It was south in every direction."

He verified his position with sextant observations, and carried out another curious proof that he was at the Pole. He believed that at the North Pole, at that time of the year, the length of a shadow should be the same for all twenty-four hours of the day. So he cut a little circle in the snow, and told the Eskimo Etukishook to stand in it. At midnight, Cook marked the place on the ice where his shadow ended. Every hour on the hour, Etukishook had to climb back into the circle while Cook marked off his shadow. Why Cook put the Eskimo through such a chore, instead of simply sticking a pole in the ice and measuring its shadow, he never explained. But after twenty-four such observations, Cook concluded that the shadows had in fact been the same length all day, because "only at the Pole is the sun of nearly equal altitude at all times of day when above the horizon."

Now began the southward journey. Fog closed in, and Cook lost his earlier trail. The food supply ran low. The Arctic summer was arriving, and the ice fields began to break up. The ice drifted steadily westward, carrying them away from their depot at Cape Thomas Hubbard. For twenty days they wandered in a gray blanket of fog, hopelessly lost. "Some advance was made nearly every day," Cook wrote, "but the cost of the desperate effort pressed life to the verge of extinction." On re-   127 duced rations, they straggled onward, missing their route by many miles. When the fog cleared, Cook took observations and found himself in latitude 79°32′N., longitude 101°22′W. "At last I had discovered our whereabouts," he wrote. "We were indeed far from where we ought to be. . . . We were in Crown Prince Gustav Sea. To the east were the low mountains and high valleys of Axel Heiberg Land. . . . Between us and the land lay fifty miles of small crushed ice and impassable lines of open water. . . ."

Cook said that he reached the low-lying Ringnes Islands, rested there a while, and pushed southward at a slow pace, killing bears for food, and eating the dogs when no other food could be had. The short summer ended; early September saw Cook and his two Eskimos at Cape Sparbo, three hundred miles from Annoatok. They decided to spend the winter there. An old Eskimo stone house served them for shelter; they hunted bear, wolf, and musk-ox for food. Laying in a supply of provisions, they settled in for the long night.

The sun returned on February 11, 1909. They readied themselves for the last leg of their journey, and reached Greenland on April 15. Three days later, they came trudging into Annoatok. An American sportsman named Harry Payne Whitney, who had accompanied Peary to the Arctic, was there. "Human beings could not be more unkempt," Whitney said. "They were half-starved and very thin, terribly dirty, and Dr. Cook, like the Eskimos, had long hair reaching to his shoulders."

Cook told Whitney that he had reached the North Pole during his fourteen months of wandering. Whitney told Cook that Peary was now somewhere to the north, in quest of the same goal.

Peary's expedition had at last sailed for the Arctic in July, 1908—three months after Cook's alleged conquest of the Pole. He called at Etah, Greenland, to pick up Eskimos and dogs, then set up a land base at Cape Columbia, to the north. At the end of February, 1909, Peary set out with twenty-four men and nineteen sledges. Cold weather and stretches of open water slowed him, but he covered 280 miles in the first month. One by one, Peary's supporting parties turned back, as was planned. When Peary got to 87°46′N., the last supporting party, headed by his Newfoundland-born friend, Captain Bob Bartlett, turned back. Peary went on, accompanied by four Eskimos and his Negro personal assistant, Matthew Henson, who had been with him on all his earlier expeditions.

Peary has been much criticized for sending Bartlett back. His enemies claimed that Peary wanted to be the first white man to reach the Pole, and did not want to share the honor with Bartlett, who was not an American citizen. The Eskimos and Henson, so it was said, "did not count" in Peary's eyes because they were of "inferior" races. Peary himself disclaimed any racist beliefs, but did say that "the Pole was something to which I had devoted my life. . . . I did not feel that under those circumstances I was called upon to divide with a man

[Bartlett] who, no matter how able and deserving he might be, was a young man and had only put a few years in that kind of work, and who had, frankly, as I believed, not the right that I had to it."

As he made his poleward dash, Peary had no idea where Cook was. It was now March, 1909. Cook had not been heard from since February, 1908. Peary believed that Cook had perished, and that he would be the first to attain the Pole. When he parted from Bartlett, Peary was 133 miles from the Pole. In a fierce spurt, he covered that distance in five days of sledging, finally reaching the Pole on April 6, 1909, exhausted and in "a daze." The four nights he had spent en route had been nearly sleepless.

"The Pole at last," Peary wrote. "The prize of three centuries. My dream and goal for twenty years. Mine at last! I cannot bring myself to realize it. It seems all so simple and commonplace."

The worldwide excitement did not begin until September 1, 1909. On that day, Dr. Cook sent a telegram from the Shetland Islands, north of Great Britain, to the New York *Herald,* the newspaper that had bought exclusive rights to his story. "Reached North Pole April 21, 1908," Cook wired. "Discovered land far north." He said that he was on his way to Copenhagen, Denmark, aboard the steamer *Hans Egede.*

The news astounded the world. No one had heard
from the rival explorers for months. Many believed that

Dr. Frederick Albert Cook had died. Peary, too, had kept silent since his return from the Pole to Greenland in late April.

On September 2, the *Herald* ran a seven-column head-line:

THE NORTH POLE IS DISCOVERED BY DR. FREDERICK A. COOK, WHO CABLES TO THE HER-ALD AN EXCLUSIVE ACCOUNT OF HOW HE SET THE AMERICAN FLAG ON THE WORLD'S TOP

Cook's story, in short, punchy newspaper paragraphs, began in this fashion:

"After a prolonged fight against famine and frost we have succeeded in reaching the North Pole.

"A new highway, with an interesting strip of animated nature, has been explored.

"Big game haunts were located which will delight the sportsman and extend the Eskimo horizon.

"A triangle of 30,000 square miles has been cut out of the terrestrial unknown."

The acclaim was all but universal. A. W. Greely, who had nearly lost his life on a polar expedition a quarter of a century before, called Cook's trip "the most ex-traordinary feat in polar exploration." Herbert L. Bridg-man, an important Peary backer, called Cook "the Co-lumbus of the Arctic." Even Mrs. Peary, who had heard no word from her husband, was generous enough to say, 131

"If Dr. Cook has found the Pole, I most certainly extend my heartiest congratulations."

But the New York *Times* sounded a slightly different note. The *Times* had paid four thousand dollars for the rights to Peary's story. It was not happy with the thought that Cook had stolen Peary's thunder. So it ran a modest one-column headline:

COOK REPORTS

HE HAS FOUND

THE NORTH POLE

Inside, a *Times* editorial cautiously wondered, "Has Man Reached the Pole?" Nearly six hundred expeditions had sought the Pole since 1800. The *Times* wanted some concrete proof from Cook before it conceded that he had really triumphed.

Cook arrived in Copenhagen on September 4, and enjoyed a royal reception. The Danish king greeted him, Danish scientists honored him, and reporters hurried from all over the world to interview him. In the midst of the uproar, there were a few doubters. Peter Freuchen, a Danish reporter who later would become famous as an explorer and writer, listened to Cook's statements and "after the first few minutes" he "was convinced that something was seriously wrong with his story." He wrote an article for his newspaper, expressing his doubts, but it was turned down. His editor explained, one "cannot wine and dine a man and at the same time call him a 132 fraud."

Another skeptic was Philip Gibbs of the London *Daily Chronicle.* Gibbs liked Cook's appearance—"hard, simple, and true"—but quickly became suspicious of his actions. He saw Cook emerge from a conversation with the crown prince of Denmark, and, wrote Gibbs, "I never saw guilt and fear more clearly written on any man's face."

On September 6, 1909, at the height of the clamor of acclaim for Cook, came a bombshell from Peary: a telegram declaring, "Stars and Stripes nailed to the Pole." Cook immediately offered his congratulations: "Glad Peary did it. Two records are better than one and more work over an easterly route has added value."

Peary had sent his message from Indian Harbor, Labrador. While there, he learned of the worldwide excitement over Cook, and realized at last that he was being regarded as the second man to the Pole—in Peary's eyes, no honor at all. On September 8, he sent a second telegram to the United Press: "Cook's story shouldn't be taken too seriously. Two Eskimos who accompanied him say he went no distance north and not out of sight of land." And he wired the *Times,* "Do not trouble about Cook's story. . . . He has simply handed the public a gold brick."

The controversy exploded devastatingly. One great explorer had publicly called another a liar. Who was telling the truth? Cook stuck to his story, and expressed pity for Peary, who should have to stoop to such base and unfounded accusations. When Cook reached New York, 133 hundreds of thousands of people turned out to hail him as a hero.

All during September, Cook and Peary traded charges. A good segment of the public was on Cook's side. Peary, that stiff, unbending, austere man, seemed pompous and arrogant. Cook, mild-mannered and friendly, seemed gentle and easy to like, and many felt that Peary was unfairly trying to rob him of his glory. The Pittsburgh *Press* took a poll whose results were published on September 26. The final tabulation showed the following figures:

Cook discovered North Pole in 1908	73,238
Peary discovered North Pole in 1909	2,814
Cook did not reach North Pole	2,814
Peary did not reach North Pole	58,009

The newspaper found the fourth line the strangest of all, since no one then had accused Peary of a hoax. "It is natural that more votes should have been cast for Cook than for Peary, because Cook had the happy faculty of making friends and inspiring confidence wherever he went," the paper commented, "and, besides, the champions of the 'underdog' in any crowd are always more vociferous. But the curious thing about it is that 58,009 persons should believe that Peary did not reach the Pole merely because he had treated [Cook] ungraciously. . . ."

It was, as the *Wall Street Journal* commented, a hot
134 argument about a cold subject. The New York *World*

declared, "The question used to be, what lies about the North Pole? Now it is, who lies about it?"

The attack on Cook's story began. Peary said that he had questioned Cook's Eskimos, Etukishook and Ahwelah, and they told stories contradicting Cook's. They said that they had never been far north at all, and never out of sight of land.

There seemed to be some inconsistencies in Cook's astronomical reports, too. He had claimed to have seen the sun at midnight for the first time on April 7. An astronomer named Stockwell pointed out that if Cook had been as far north as he claimed, the midnight sun should have been visible from April 1 on. Cook's answer was that there must have been clouds and haze hiding the sun until the seventh—but in a later book, Cook juggled his dates around to make them fit Stockwell's objections.

George Kennan, an explorer and writer, did some calculating on the subject of Cook's food supply, and pointed out that by Cook's own figures he must have run out of food on May 2, but he did not reach land until June 13. What did he and the two Eskimos eat during those six weeks? Cook's answers only led him into new inconsistencies.

And what were the "instruments" with which Cook claimed to have observed his approach of the Pole? In 1908, there were no instruments that could exactly locate the North Pole. Cook did not explain.

It was at this time that Ed Barrille and other members of Cook's 1906 Mount McKinley expedition publicly accused him of having faked his climb to the summit of that mountain. By implication, he had also faked his polar journey. So Cook found himself fighting two battles at once. His moment of triumph had turned into nightmare. Harried and mocked, exhausted by the endless questioning to which he was being submitted, Cook simply disappeared. Wild rumors arose. His brother feared that Cook had been murdered by Peary supporters while "hurrying to Copenhagen with proofs of having found the North Pole." Walter Lonsdale, Cook's secretary, talked of "spies" following Cook, and spoke darkly of assassination plots. These stories indicate the mental condition of Cook and his friends at the time; they saw enemies lurking under every bush.

The various learned bodies of the geographical world were still waiting for proof. The University of Copenhagen appointed a committee to study the Cook claims; the National Geographic Society, on October 1, 1909, said it could accept "the personal statements of neither Commander Peary nor Dr. Cook that the Pole had been reached, without investigation by its Committee on Research or by a scientific body acceptable to it." It urged both men to submit documentation of their trips.

On December 21, the Copenhagen group issued its verdict. Cook had submitted nothing but a report of his journey, and a typed copy of his notebooks. There were no astronomical observations, no scientific data. The committee decided that there was not sufficient proof to credit Cook with attainment of the North Pole.

The public's attitude toward Cook began to change. There was too much evidence against him, and his wild talk of spies and assassins did not help his reputation. It began to seem certain that he had invented his whole journey for the sake of publicity.

Peary, meanwhile, was trying to prove *his* polar trip had really taken place. It was not so easy. He had no witnesses except for Henson, his own employee. The North Pole is not a fixed place where records can be deposited; the ice pack that had covered the Pole in 1909 had broken up and moved away. When Amundsen reached the South Pole in 1911, he left a flag there that was found soon afterward by Robert Scott, the second conqueror of the heart of the Antarctic. But Peary could offer only his word and his scientific records, which were skimpy.

He submitted his records to the National Geographic Society, which reported itself "unanimously of the opinion that Commander Peary reached the North Pole on April 6, 1909." But the National Geographic Society had donated money for Peary's expedition, so it could be challenged as not impartial. And some of the records of Peary's trip looked odd. He had claimed to have marched forty-five miles on each of his last two days. Other Arctic explorers had rarely done better than twenty or twenty-five miles a day. Could Peary's seemingly fantastic pace be accepted?

There were those who said no—though Vilhjalmur Stefansson, the Arctic expert, found Peary's mileage 137 "reasonable." Stefansson noted that if Peary had been faking, he would have deliberately delayed his return to avoid just such charges.

In the long run, Peary's claim was accepted, chiefly on the basis of the character of Peary the man. No one could believe that Peary was capable of lying. As Roald Amundsen put it, "What you say about his ability to fake his observations is perfectly true. The answer to any doubt on that score is simply that Peary was not that sort of man." Donald B. MacMillan, a member of Peary's expedition, said, "I know that Admiral Peary reached the Pole. . . . The character of the explorer . . . is always the best evidence of his claim. . . . We have his word."

Still, many of Peary's observations have been overthrown by later exploration. He claimed to have seen land, which he called Crocker Land, but no one else has ever been able to find it. (Cook's Bradley Land also turned out to be nonexistent.) Many of Peary's landmarks were eliminated from United States Navy charts in 1916 when they were found by other explorers not to exist. Such errors of observation, though, are easy to make under polar conditions, and many another explorer of unquestioned authenticity has committed similar mistakes.

Peary is generally credited today with being the first man to reach the North Pole—though there remains a small party of students clinging to the belief that neither 138 Peary nor Cook ever reached the Pole, and that the first man to see it was Richard E. Byrd, who flew over it in 1926.

Cook still has his backers, also. It is interesting to note that many of the people who believe in the honesty of Dr. Cook also firmly believe in the genuineness of such things as the Kensington Stone. Evidently they have a psychological need to rebel against commonly accepted scientific opinions. If the general belief is that Cook was a fraud and the Kensington Stone another, they warmly defend the authenticity of both. They cling to their beliefs even if it is necessary to close their eyes to a great deal of evidence.

The case against Dr. Cook grew worse and worse as the years went by. By 1913, Hudson Stuck had shown that Cook had lied about Mount McKinley. Between 1913 and 1918, Vilhjalmur Stefansson explored much of the region where Cook claimed to have been in the Arctic, and found that it did not at all match Cook's descriptions.

Stefansson and others felt that Cook never tried to go north of Cape Thomas Hubbard, perhaps finding the weather too severe. Instead, they argued, he traveled south along the west coast of Axel Heiberg Island, made camp for the winter, and headed back for Greenland in the spring of 1909. Why he claimed to have reached the North Pole is anybody's guess. Perhaps something happened to Cook's mind during the dark, terrible winter he spent in the Antarctic aboard the *Belgica* in 1898–99. Until then, he seems to have been a thoroughly admirable character; after his return from Antarctica, we find

139

him stealing dictionaries, lying about Mount McKinley, and finally inventing his conquest of the North Pole.

Cook spent the remaining years of his life trying to clear his reputation. He toured the country, lecturing to all who would listen. Luckily for him, he had several wealthy backers who believed his story, and they helped him along.

But he ran into new troubles in 1923. He had become involved with a company called the Petroleum Producers' Association, whose main activity was to exchange its stock for the shares of oil companies that were in bad financial shape. Cook and his business associates claimed that the P.P.A. oil land would one day spout a bonanza of oil.

It was a time of wild stock speculation, and many another shady promoter was allowed to get away with such operations. Not Cook. He and nineteen confederates were indicted and tried in Texas on charges of using the mails to defraud. Six pleaded guilty and got off with light sentences. Of the fourteen who were tried, most received short sentences, but the judge threw the book at Dr. Cook: fourteen years and nine months in prison, and a twelve-thousand-dollar fine. It was an extraordinary punishment for the charge, and there were those who felt that Cook was simply being punished for his earlier hoaxes, which had not, of course, violated any criminal laws.

In 1925, Cook entered the federal penitentiary at Leavenworth, Kansas. He was a model prisoner, editing the prison newspaper, working in the prison hospital, and occupying himself with philosophical writings and fanciful schemes for curing baldness and air-conditioning large cities. Ironically, while he was in prison the land owned by the Petroleum Producers' Association began yielding oil, millions of dollars' worth—but Cook no longer owned it.

Cook was given a parole in 1930, when he was sixty-five years old. Few people had thought much about him during his years in prison, though his old Antarctic companion, Roald Amundsen, had visited him at Leavenworth. Amundsen, who felt that Peary had reached the Pole and Cook had not, still was fond of the troubled doctor. "I am wholly unfamiliar with the facts which led to his imprisonment," Amundsen wrote, "and I have no desire to know them. . . . Whatever Cook may have done, the Cook who did them was not the Dr. Cook I knew as a young man, the soul of honor and kindliness, lion-hearted in courage. Some physical misfortune must have overtaken him to change his personality, for which he was not responsible."

Once again a free man, Cook renewed his attempt to clear his name. He filed suit against a number of writers and publishers who had cast doubt on his polar exploit, but none of the suits ever came to trial. In old age, his sight began to fail, and then his health. He suffered a stroke in 1940, and, as he lay close to death, President Franklin D. Roosevelt granted Cook a full pardon on the mail-fraud conviction. The controversial explorer died a few days later, on August 5, 1940. He had outlived Peary by twenty years, and had outlived his own reputation as an honest man by thirty.

Cook still has his champions. On April 21, 1958, the fiftieth anniversary of Cook's alleged attainment of the Pole, Representative John R. Pillion, a conservative Republican congressman from New York, took the floor of Congress to praise Cook for his "discovery." Mysteriously, Dr. Cook has become a hero of the extreme right wing of American politics. He is regarded by some rightists as a victim of a left-wing conspiracy to give the credit to Peary.

Cook's gentleness, his unfailing courtesy in the face of bitter attack, his apparent modesty and humility, won him many friends. The champions of lost causes find him easy to love. Peary, on the other hand, was as frosty as his oft-explored Arctic. Great as his accomplishments were, he made many enemies through his brusqueness and self-willed nature, and through the ferocity of his attack on Cook.

All these factors, though, are beside the point. The evidence indicates that Cook perpetrated a fantastic fraud and that Peary made a great journey of exploration. The last word, perhaps, was spoken by the explorer Peter Freuchen.

"Cook," Freuchen said, "was a liar and a gentleman. Peary was neither."

8: *Paul Schliemann and the Lost Continent of Atlantis*

It is a terribly frustrating thing to be the unimportant relative of a famous man. All your life you are haunted by the accomplishments of your celebrated ancestor. You tell people your name, and then you wait tensely for the inevitable question, "Oh, are you related to ———?"

Some men are able to win fame in their own right. The son of President John Adams became President himself—John Quincy Adams. President Benjamin Harrison was the grandson of President William Henry

Harrison. The son of the writer Alexandre Dumas was also a famous writer (though never quite as famous as his father). Douglas Fairbanks, Jr., followed his father's path to Hollywood stardom.

But one who never matched his grandfather's achievements was Paul Schliemann, grandson of the great archaeologist Heinrich Schliemann. The elder Schliemann was a remarkable man. Penniless at nineteen, he made use of his unusual gift for languages to build a successful business career, and by the time he was thirty-three he was not only a millionaire but was fluent in fifteen languages. Archaeology was his great passion, and Homer's Troy his chief obsession. At the age of forty-six, Heinrich Schliemann retired from business and went in search of Troy.

Most authorities then felt—it was 1868—that Homer's poems were pure fantasy, and that there had never been any city of Troy. Schliemann, with the lines of the *Iliad* blazing in his mind, dug into a hill called Hissarlik in Asia Minor, found not one buried city but seven, one atop the other, uncovered fabulous golden treasures, and forced the experts to agree that he had indeed rediscovered Troy. He went on to excavate at Mycenae, the city of King Agamemnon, and at other ancient Greek sites. At his death in 1890, Schliemann was planning to unearth Knossos, the fabulous capital of King Minos of Crete, but that prize fell to another man, Arthur Evans.

Paul Schliemann was the unimportant grandson of
144 this very important man. All Europe knew the name of

Schliemann. The grandson had only to mention the name, and he would draw the response, "Ah, yes. Are you related to the Schliemann who dug up Troy?" It became irksome. Young Paul Schliemann looked about for some way to establish his own reputation, but, unfortunately, he seems not to have had his grandfather's abilities either as an archaeologist or as a scholar. So he made his mark on the world in another way.

On October 20, 1912, the New York *American* published a long article under the by-line of Dr. Paul Schliemann. The *American* belonged to William Randolph Hearst, and its specialty was the sensational and the flamboyant. It was not precisely a scholarly journal.

Schliemann's article was headed, "How I Discovered Atlantis, the Source of All Civilization." He did not claim that he had actually discovered the site of the fabled lost continent for which men had searched so long. He merely let it be known that he was in possession of definite proof that Atlantis had really existed. Just as men once had called Troy a myth, so too did they still regard Atlantis as imaginary. But Paul Schliemann assured the readers of the New York *American* that the lost continent was no myth. His authority for the statement, he said, was no one else than his illustrious grandfather, the discoverer of Troy, Heinrich Schliemann.

Paul Schliemann wrote:

"A few days before my grandfather, Dr. Heinrich Schliemann, passed away at Naples, Italy, in 1890, he gave a heavy sealed envelope to one of his closest 145 friends. This envelope was marked: 'To be opened only by a member of my own family, if he pledges himself to devote all his life to the work sketched herein.'

"Only one hour before his death he asked for paper and pencil and wrote with trembling hands: 'Secret addition to the contents of the sealed envelope: Break the owl-headed vase. Study its contents. They refer to Atlantis. Excavate east of the ruins of the Temple of Sais and among the tombs in Chacuna Valley. Important! You'll find proof of my theories. Darkness is coming fast—farewell!'

"He then ordered that this message also be delivered to his friend, who deposited it in the vaults of a French banking firm. After I had studied for several years in Russia, Germany, and the near Orient I decided to continue the work begun by my famous grandsire.

"In 1906 I gave the pledge and broke the seals of the letter. It contained numerous photographs and documents. The first of them was marked: 'Whoever opens this has to pledge himself to finish the work I had to leave unfinished. . . . I deposited a sum of money that will be sufficient to finish the work in a French bank. The money is at the disposal of the person that shows the enclosed receipt.' "

Paul Schliemann told of his painstaking research. He traced the owl-headed vase among his grandfather's huge collection, and broke it open. Inside, he said, he discovered some unusual square coins made of an alloy 146 of platinum, aluminum, and silver. There was also a

square piece of silvery-looking metal that bore the inscription in Phoenician characters, "Issued in the Temple of the Transparent Walls."

Schliemann pointed out that the inscribed metal
plaque was much larger than the diameter of the vase's
neck. He had no idea how it had been put inside the
vase. There were other curious things in the vase, too,
objects made from pieces of fossilized bone and from
clay. Many of them bore the inscription, in Phoenician,
"From the King Cronos of Atlantis."

Atlantis! "You can imagine my excitement," Schliemann wrote. "Here was the first material evidence of
that great continent whose legend has lived for ages!"

The article went on to say that Heinrich Schliemann
had examined certain vases, bone objects, and pottery
artifacts at the Louvre, in Paris, that had come from
Tiahuanaco in the southern highlands of Peru. And, said
Paul Schliemann, his grandfather had discovered that
the Tiahuanaco relics were identical in every respect to
the "Atlantis" relics supposedly found at Troy. The only
difference was that the Peruvian material lacked the
Phoenician inscriptions that mentioned Atlantis.

By bringing Tiahuanaco into the story, Paul Schliemann added a fresh aspect of mystery. Tiahuanaco is a
valley about thirteen thousand feet high, in the Peruvian
Andes. It is bleak, forbidding country there, nearly tree-
less, eternally cold.

Strange monuments are found at Tiahuanaco. Strangest of all is the Gateway of the Sun, a vast gate standing   147

alone and leading nowhere. It is carved from a ten-ton block of lava, and is twelve and a half feet wide, ten feet high. A doorway cut in its center is surrounded by weird, alien-looking carvings of bizarre figures. Nearby is a triangular stone pyramid, fifty feet high and almost seven hundred feet along each side; there is also a stone courtyard more than four hundred feet square, and a red sandstone figure twenty-four feet high. All this is eerie and even frightening amid the desolate surroundings.

Modern archaeologists think that the Tiahuanaco monuments are the work of Peruvian Indians who built them before A.D. 1000, several centuries prior to the Inca conquest of Peru. But, because of their unusual and almost unearthly style, the Tiahuanaco ruins have been the subject of many fanciful theories. Some imaginative people see Tiahuanaco as the site of a settlement of beings from space; others claim it is the place where mankind originated. There are those who say that Tiahuanaco once was a Pacific island, lifted to its present great height by some colossal upheaval of the earth. Some think that its monuments are akin to those of ancient Egypt.

Along came Paul Schliemann now to suggest that Tiahuanaco was the place where the people of Atlantis settled after the destruction of their continent. The so-called "Egyptian" features that many people claimed to see in the Tiahuanaco monuments, Schliemann said, could be explained by the fact that some Atlanteans had gone to Egypt and others to Peru. That was why such widely

148

separated parts of the world seemed to have an art style in common.

The younger Schliemann claimed that he had devoted the years from 1906 to 1912 to an intensive program of research. He said he had been to Peru and Egypt, to the Mayan ruins of Central America, and to archaeological museums all over the world. He asserted that a Buddhist temple at Lhasa, Tibet, had supplied him with a four-thousand-year-old Chaldean (Babylonian) manuscript telling how the Land of the Seven Cities—Atlantis, apparently—had been destroyed by earthquake and volcanic eruption after the star Bel fell to earth. According to the manuscript, "Mu, the priest of Ra" had warned the Atlanteans of their fate, but they had refused to listen in time. Only a handful of the doomed continent's people had escaped to Egypt and to South America when the cataclysm occurred.

Schliemann let it be known that he was still at work on the mystery of Atlantis, and soon would publish a book giving further details. "But if I desired to say everything I know," he concluded, "there would be no more mystery about it." The archaeological discovery of Atlantis, he implied, would soon take place, thus ending thousands of years of speculation and controversy about the "lost continent."

The Atlantis story goes back to about 355 B.C. The philosopher Plato, then in his seventies, was nearing the end of his career. His great teacher Socrates had been dead for forty-five years, but Plato had kept Socrates' name alive in a series of literary works, the Socratic dialogues, which used Socrates as a character in dramatic sketches of philosophical debate.

Late in his life Plato wrote a dialogue called *Timaeus,* which was set in 421 B.C., when Socrates had been about fifty and Plato himself only a boy. The chief characters of the dialogue are Socrates and two of his friends, Timaeus and Critias. At one point in the discussion, Critias tells the story of Atlantis, which he says has been handed down in his family since the time of his great-grandfather Dropides.

Dropides, Critias says, had known Solon, the famous lawgiver of Athens. In about 550 B.C., Solon had visited Egypt and had spoken with the priests of Sais, a city at the head of the Nile Delta. Solon had begun to tell the priests some legends of early Greek history, but the priests had laughed at him. "You do not even know your own history," they told Solon. "Your records have been destroyed by fire and flood." Only in Egypt had the true accounts of ancient days been reserved, and the Egyptians knew stories of Athens' greatness in the remote past.

Solon begged for details, so Critias says. The Egyptian priests told him how Athens had been great as far back as nine thousand years before: "Many great and wonderful deeds are recorded of your state in our histories. But one of them exceeds all the rest in greatness and valor." A mighty enemy had come out of the Atlantic, entering the Mediterranean between the Pillars of Hercules (today the Strait of Gibraltar). These invaders came from an island larger than Asia and Africa put together, called Atlantis.

The Atlanteans tried to subdue Greece and Egypt and all the other countries of the world. "And then, Solon," said the priests, "your country shone forth. . . . Being compelled to stand alone, she defeated and triumphed over the invaders." Soon after this great victory, "there occurred violent earthquakes and floods, and in a single day and night of rain . . . the island of Atlantis disappeared, and was sunk beneath the sea." That explained why the Atlantic was so shallow and muddy beyond the Pillars of Hercules—for lost Atlantis lay just beneath the waves.

Solon, returning to Athens, had told the story of Atlantis to Dropides, who wrote it down and passed it to his descendants. "My great-grandfather, Dropides, had the original writing, which is still in my possession," Critias declares. And Socrates comments, "This is no invented fable but genuine history."

In a second dialogue, *Critias*, Plato provided some further details about this continent that supposedly had been destroyed nine thousand years before his time. It had been, he declared, a place of great splendor and wealth, with soaring palaces and vast canals and majestic bridges. One temple, six hundred feet long and three hundred feet wide, was entirely covered by silver, and its roof was of gold. Within, the ceiling was fashioned from 151 ivory inlaid with silver and gold. There were gardens, racecourses, parks, superb harbors thronged with ships, and wealth beyond measure. And all this had gone to the bottom of the sea in a single day and night.

Plato had simply been telling a pretty story. He had always been a gifted and imaginative writer, and, since it had suited his philosophical purposes to speak of Athens' past grandeur, he had invented glorious Atlantis —which he said Athens had conquered. Neither Plato nor the Egyptian priests at Sais had any real information about events of 9500 B.C.; in actuality, Egypt herself was still a primitive land then, and Athens was unknown.

The fictitious nature of Plato's Atlantis was made evident by a remark of his one-time pupil, Aristotle. Speaking of Plato and Atlantis, Aristotle said, "He who invented it also destroyed it." But the appeal of Plato's imaginary palaces and gold-roofed temples was powerful. Two hundred years after Aristotle, a friend of Cicero's named Poseidonius wrote, "It is possible that the story about the island of Atlantis is not a fiction." Gradually Atlantis began to pass from fiction into fact. Plato's fanciful story was taken at face value.

The great surge of exploration that began in the fifteenth and sixteenth centuries saw many men out looking for Atlantis. Some said that the scattered islands of the Caribbean were the remains of the lost continent, though they were far from the Pillars of Hercules. When Euro-
152 peans reached South and Central America and found the

highly developed civilizations of the Aztecs, Incas, and Maya, the question arose of whether they had descended from refugees escaping the destruction of Atlantis. That idea took firm hold.

The Spanish *conquistadores* shattered those three great civilizations before much could be learned about them. One of those who helped in the destruction was Diego de Landa, Bishop of Yucatán. Landa, convinced that the books of the Maya Indians were works of the devil, rounded up all he could find and burned them, in the middle of the sixteenth century. He did, however, take the trouble to make a record, inaccurate and confused, of the Mayan alphabet.

Diego de Landa's book remained unknown, hidden away in a Spanish library, until 1864, when a French scholar stumbled across the bishop's dusty manuscript. This man, Charles-Etienne Brasseur, immediately tried to decipher one of the few Mayan books that had survived Landa's bonfire.

He emerged with an absurd-sounding description of a volcanic eruption. It began, "The master is he of the upheaved earth, the master of the calabash, the earth upheaved of the tawny beast (at the place engulfed beneath the floods)—it is he, the master of the upheaved earth, of the swollen earth, beyond measure, he the master . . . of the basin of water."

Not content with this gibberish, Brasseur provided another scholarly contribution. Going over the Mayan text, he found two symbols for which he could not account.   153

They vaguely resembled the letters M and U of Landa's incorrect Mayan alphabet. Brasseur decided that they must be the name of the land destroyed by the eruption: Mu.

All his findings are known today to be nonsense. The Mayan book Brasseur "translated" is actually a treatise on Mayan astrology, not a description of a volcanic eruption. And Bishop de Landa's alphabetical interpretations were mostly wrong, though he did set down authentic Mayan letters.

Brasseur's work, however, inspired another French pseudoscientist to carry the quest for Mu—the Atlantis of Plato—a step further. He was Augustus le Plongeon (1826–1908), a physician who lived in Mexico. Le Plongeon visited the Mayan ruins in Yucatán, which had been discovered in the middle of the nineteenth century. and found on the walls of the temples of the Mayan city of Chichen-Itza pictures that struck him as a portrayal of the destruction of Atlantis. Using Brasseur's translation of the Mayan text, and adding some interpretations of his own, Le Plongeon came up with this account of the catastrophe:

"In the year 6 Kan, on the 11th Muluc in the month Zac, there occurred terrible earthquakes, which continued without interruption until the 13th Chuen. The country of the hills of mud, the land of Mu was sacrificed: being twice upheaved it suddenly disappeared during the night, the basin being continually shaken by the volcanic forces. Being confined, these caused the land to sink and to rise several times in various places. At last the surface gave way and ten countries were torn asunder and scattered. Unable to stand the force of the convulsion, they sank with their 64,000,000 inhabitants 8060 years before the writing of this book."

Le Plongeon also claimed to have found and translated a romantic tale of the love of Prince Coh and his brother Prince Aac for Queen Moo of Mu. Prince Coh was successful in winning Queen Moo's hand, but was murdered by the disappointed Prince Aac, who seized the throne from Queen Moo. Then the earthquake struck, and the continent of Mu went under. Queen Moo managed to escape to Egypt, where she built the Sphinx as a monument to Prince Coh, and founded the Egyptian civilization. Other Muvians reached Central America and became known as the Mayas.

No doubt the fantasies of Brasseur and Le Plongeon were familiar to Paul Schliemann when he wrote his newspaper piece in 1912. He rolled everything into one superfantasy—Atlantis, Mu, Plato, Le Plongeon, the Mayas, Tiahuanaco, the Phoenicians, and much else— and tied it all up by linking it to his grandfather's work at Troy.

Respectable scientists had been laughing at Brasseur, Le Plongeon, and other advocates of Atlantis for years. But suddenly a man bearing the revered name of Schliemann had appeared, insisting he had proof that Atlantis really had existed. The experts were startled. Had Hein- 155 rich Schliemann really discovered references to Atlantis during his excavations at Troy? Or would Paul Schliemann dare to take his grandfather's name in vain, by shamelessly dragging him into a hoax?

The first reaction to Paul Schliemann's article, therefore, was one of surprise but not of scorn. Then the experts began to look a little more closely at the story.

Paul Schliemann's mention of a temple in Tibet aroused suspicion. Many of the wilder proponents of Atlantis had included Tibet in their fantasies, because it was a remote and mysterious place well suited to enhancing an occult story. How had Schliemann made contact with the Buddhist priests of Tibet? And where was his "Chaldean manuscript"? The Chaldeans, that is, the Babylonians, of four thousand years ago had not had "manuscripts," anyway. They had written things on tablets of clay.

Those coins and plaques made of platinum, aluminum, and silver caused trouble too. Platinum was an extremely rare metal, while aluminum in its metallic form had been unknown until the nineteenth century. Aluminum would have been virtually impossible for the ancients to produce, and no one could see why they would have gone to the bother of using it for coins.

There were other archaeologists who wondered why Heinrich Schliemann had kept his wonderful find a secret. The elder Schliemann had never been given to secrecy; on the contrary, he had usually announced every 156 important discovery right away, trumpeting it in loud, clear tones. And there were those who thought it odd that no one but Paul Schliemann had ever seen the mysterious platinum-aluminum-silver coins with the inscriptions referring to Atlantis. Nor did the curators of various museums recollect any visits from Paul Schliemann in the past six years, when he had supposedly been doing worldwide research.

Paul Schliemann remained silent while these questions were being raised. That, too, was suspicious. Still, no one branded him as a hoaxer—not yet. The checking went on.

One archaeologist, Alexander Bessmertny, went to the man most likely to know the truth: Wilhelm Dörpfeld, who had taken part in Heinrich Schliemann's excavations. Bessmertny wrote to Dörpfeld and got this answer:

"I gladly inform you that I have already been asked about the report made by Dr. Paul Schliemann, though I do not recall by whom. As far as I can remember, I replied at that time as I have to reply to you, too, that Heinrich Schliemann did not work extensively on the Atlantis problem, at least not to my knowledge. I never heard about activities concerning Atlantis from him, although I was his assistant from 1882 to 1890, the year of his death.

"It is true that we talked about Atlantis occasionally, and I think it likely that Heinrich Schliemann may have collected notes about Atlantis. But I do not believe that he carried out any work on that theme himself."

Now was the time for Paul Schliemann to come forth   157

with solid proof: the coins, the inscribed plaque, his book on Atlantis, anything. But he maintained his silence. He had nothing at all to say. The game was up. Goaded by his need to seem important, he had invented the whole story out of thin air. He had no proof. His book never appeared. This pathetic little man had his moment of public attention, and for a brief while his name was on people's lips, as once his grandfather's had been. Then he vanished back into the obscurity from which he had come. The lost continent of Atlantis remains lost today, though the noisy followers of Le Plongeon and Brasseur still think it will be discovered some day. If Plato, who loved truth above all else, had known what men would make of his airy fable, he quite probably would never have set it down for the credulous to read.

9: *The Etruscan Sculptures*

Until early in 1961, New York's Metropolitan Museum of Art was the proud possessor of three unique treasures of the past. They were enormous works of sculpture, somber and even terrifying, which had a room almost to themselves on the museum's second floor.

The sculptures dated, so the museum said, from about 500 B.C. They were products of the strange and mysterious Etruscans, a people who had lived in Italy before the rise of Rome. Two of the works were figures of fierce-looking warriors, a slender one six feet high, a massive one eight feet high. The third piece was a helmeted head of gigantic size, nearly five feet high. What made these three huge statues so important was the fact that they were the only known large works of Etruscan art.

There was only one thing wrong with the three Etruscan sculptures. They were fakes. They had been made about 1914 by three clever Italian swindlers. The Metropolitan Museum of Art, after displaying them prominently for more than forty years, suddenly discovered the embarrassing truth that it had been hoaxed.

On February 13, 1961, a Metropolitan Museum spokesman offered a sheepish statement about the Etruscan statues: he declared that they "must be considered of doubtful authenticity. . . . Modern scientific and technical analyses . . . developed convincing proof that these famous statues were not made in ancient times. . . ." With those words, the case of the Etruscan sculptures was closed. A great museum had been bamboozled, and another spectacular hoax had been added to the annals of human chicanery.

The Etruscans, the supposed creators of the three discredited statues, are one of the most puzzling peoples of the past. They present archaeologists with many baffling problems.

No one is sure, for example, of the details of their early history. About 700 B.C., we know, they were in possession of Italy, and had a highly developed culture that must have been a long time in the making. But where did they come from? How could such a complicated civilization have sprung, as it would appear, from nowhere?

The Greek historian Herodotus, writing in the fifth century B.C., said that the Etruscans had come to Italy from Asia Minor. He told a story of a mass migration from Lydia, a country of Asia Minor, after a famine that lasted eighteen years. But some four hundred years after Herodotus, another Greek historian, Dionysius of Halicarnassus, flatly contradicted that theory. "I do not think the Tyrrhenians [Etruscans] were emigrants from Lydia," Dionysius wrote. He declared that "those who say that the Etruscans are not a people who came from abroad, but are native to Italy, are right; to me this seems to follow from the fact that they are a very ancient people which does not resemble any other in its language or its customs."

The scholars are still divided today. Many believe that Herodotus' account should be accepted. But there are several important European Etruscologists who insist that the Etruscans lived in Italy from earliest times. The mystery of the Etruscans' origins may be solved by future archaeological work, but at the moment it remains an unanswerable question.

Another Etruscan problem is their language. There are about ten thousand Etruscan texts known, most of them tomb inscriptions. The Etruscan alphabet can be understood; it is adapted from the Greek alphabet, and is quite similar to our own. But the words make no sense. 161

The Etruscan language appears to be unrelated to any other. As one Etruscologist has written, "Etruscan stands apart from the various known families of languages, and it seems impossible to find a distant cousin—far less a twin."

After several centuries of research, only some thirty Etruscan words have been deciphered. The rest of the language remains unintelligible. The writing of much more ancient peoples can be understood—the Egyptians, the Babylonians, the Chinese—but Etruscan writing remains sealed and enigmatic.

We do know some Etruscan history. The Etruscans lived in the hilly, attractive central district of Italy that is called Tuscany today. Such cities as Florence, Pisa, and Siena have arisen in what was once Etruscan territory. The Etruscans were good sailors, and after about 700 B.C. they figured importantly in the Mediterranean area both as merchants and as pirates. An Etruscan empire began to spread through Italy and the surrounding lands.

Rome, at this time, was an unimportant little village. About 616 B.C., the Etruscans conquered Rome without difficulty, and an Etruscan named Tarquin became king of Rome. Under Tarquin, a great construction program turned Rome into a large, powerful city for the first time. When he was assassinated in 579, another Etruscan, Servius Tullius, took the Roman throne, and he was followed in time by Tarquin's son, Lucius Tarquin, 162 called Tarquin the Proud. In 510, Tarquin the Proud was driven into exile, and Rome became an independent republic.

Gradually the Romans gobbled up the Etruscan empire. City after city fell to the ever more mighty Rome, until by 300 B.C. only two Etruscan cities still were free. Within fifty years they too had been conquered. Etruria, the land of the Etruscans, was absorbed into Rome. Latin-speaking colonists went north to live in Etruria. The Etruscan language and customs slowly died out. By the time of Emperor Claudius, in the first century A.D., Etruscan was a dead language and scholars already were at work studying the civilization of the dethroned masters of Italy, just as in the United States we study the vanished cultures of the American Indians.

The Romans also took a special interest in Etruscan art, and for good reason. The Etruscans were master craftsmen. Their statues and paintings were magnificent works of art, vivid and exciting. With fantastic colors and strange poses, the Etruscan artists portrayed the life of their civilization in close detail. Etruscan art was marked by flamboyant style and by a kind of eerie, awe-inspiring differentness. There is something haunting and weird about the art of this long-dead culture.

Wealthy Romans in the days of the empire formed collections of Etruscan art. When Rome fell, the Etruscans were forgotten, and it was not until the sixteenth century that anyone devoted attention to them. With the coming of the Renaissance to Italy, excavations for new churches and temples produced hidden treasure troves 163 of Etruscan art. Once again it became fashionable to collect Etruscan things. Tombs were opened and found to contain superb art treasures. Thousands of Etruscan vases, urns, statues, and ornaments were put on the market and found eager buyers.

The demand for Etruscan objects was heavy, and so obliging fakers moved in to produce some up-to-date "Etruscan" treasures to sell to the ignorant. A new Italian industry was born: the manufacture of counterfeit Etruscan antiquities.

Actually, that industry was some two thousand years old. The first fake Etruscan vases were turned out in the district of Apulia during the time of Julius Caesar. But the Apulians were ignorant forgers; they made such clumsy mistakes in their attempts to copy the Etruscan alphabet that the imitations could easily be recognized by a glance at the bungled inscriptions on them.

The revival of interest in the Etruscans after the sixteenth century spurred a rebirth of the counterfeiting operation. Early in the nineteenth century, a craze for Etruscan art spread through Europe—"Etruscomania," it was called—and the forgers worked overtime to supply the market with brand-new Etruscan relics.

Many of these found their way into important museums. The British Museum paid a substantial sum for a curious-looking "Etruscan" coffin with two figures carved on its lid. In time, the museum found that its prize had been concocted about 1860 by the Pinelli brothers, a team of gifted antiquity-fakers from Rome. The phony sarcophagus was promptly hidden away in the museum's basement, along with various other fraudulent items that had come into the venerable institution's possession over the years.

The Metropolitan Museum of Art in New York began forming its Etruscan collection late in the nineteenth century. It sent agents to Europe to purchase new items that might come on the market. The Metropolitan's agent in Rome at the time of World War I was a man named John Marshall. He had a good reputation as an expert on ancient art—the sort of man, one would think, who was not likely to be easily fooled.

In 1915, an art dealer in Rome showed Marshall the broken fragments of a large statue that looked Etruscan. Marshall bought it for the Metropolitan. The following year, he was offered the pieces of an even larger statue, and he bought that too. In 1921 came the third item, the big helmeted head, also in fragments.

The shattered statues were restored in New York by the Metropolitan's experts, and went on exhibit in the Etruscan halls of the museum, with a date of 500 B.C. In 1933, Gisela M. A. Richter, then the museum's curator of classical art, published a study of the three statues in which she declared them to be undoubtedly genuine. Four years later, she wrote a second essay on them, repeating her earlier conclusions. This time she was joined by Charles F. Binns of Harvard, who examined the statues minutely. Binns declared that they were covered with   165 a kind of glaze known as "Greek black," the secret of which had been lost during the time of the Roman Empire. That seemed certain proof that the museum's statues were genuinely ancient.

But some of the experts had their doubts, all the same.

One of the skeptics was Massimo Pallotino of the University of Rome, a leading Etruscologist. In 1937, Pallotino wrote an article attacking the Metropolitan's three statues as modern and fraudulent. Other authorities, chiefly in Italy, shared Dr. Pallotino's opinion. One of them was Professor Pico Cellini of Rome, who declared in 1955 that the three statues were fakes. He also denounced an Etruscan "throne" owned by the Boston Museum of Fine Arts, which was later unmasked as a forgery made in 1894.

The man who provided the finishing touch for the big "Etruscan" statues was not a professional Etruscologist at all. He was Boston-born Harold Woodbury Parsons, who not only exposed the fraud but produced the hoaxer.

Parsons had studied science at Harvard about the turn of the century, but had then become interested in art. He had served as European buying agent for a number of American art museums, including those of Cleveland, Kansas City, and Omaha. In 1960, the seventy-eight-year-old Parsons was living in retirement in Rome when he heard rumors that a certain elderly repairman of antiques and jewelry knew something about counterfeit

166   Etruscan art.

Parsons sought him out. The man's name was Alfredo Fioravanti, and he was the same age as Parsons, seventy-eight. Parsons became friendly with the mild-looking, bespectacled Fioravanti, and eventually won his confidence. Fioravanti then confessed his part in the manufacture of the Metropolitan Museum's trio of Etruscan sculptures.

Those three works of art had always struck Parsons as fakes. "I sensed something wrong," he said, after viewing them. He did not feel that they were in the true Etruscan style. Parsons called "their ferocious gestures static, their faces but deathlike masks." He wrote, "They could not possibly roll their eyeballs or unstick their frozen lips or flex a muscle: they are lifeless." He compared them with an undoubtedly genuine Etruscan statue, the "Apollo" found in Veii, which he said was "alive with tense energy and has convincing structure. . . . His lips part, his nostrils distend, his eyes roll, his hair lifts with the breeze."

Fioravanti now proceeded to confirm all of Parsons' suspicions. This was the story he told.

Originally, Fioravanti had been a tailor. But early in this century he met two brothers named Riccardi, who were in the business of mending ancient pottery for Italian antique dealers. Fioravanti found the trade more interesting than patching clothes, so he took a job with them.

He had a knack for the work, and became skillful at it. The business thrived. One day an idea occurred to one 167 of the Riccardi brothers. Instead of simply repairing antiquities, why not produce them and sell them? How much more profitable it would be, he said, to employ their skills that way!

They began cautiously, making fragments rather than complete pieces. Art dealers bought them without question. They went on to making small complete pieces, vases and little statues. Then, in 1914, they turned to a more ambitious task.

Fioravanti and the two brothers, working in the ancient city of Orvieto—once an Etruscan metropolis—obtained clay of the same sort the Etruscans themselves had used for their statues. They built a large standing warrior, taking as their model a photo of a small statue now in a Berlin museum. The figure was so large that they could not bake the clay in their little kiln, so they had to break the statue into fragments and fire each piece separately. They smeared the fragments with mud to make them look ancient, and turned them over to an art dealer who is now dead. He, in turn, sold them to John Marshall, the agent for the Metropolitan Museum.

The amount that Marshall paid has never been disclosed. Fioravanti thought that it might have been as much as forty thousand dollars. "But all we got was a few hundred," Fioravanti told Parsons. Still, it was good pay for the effort involved, and they immediately began work on an even larger statue of the same sort. Their model this time was a photo of a figure on the Etruscan sarcophagus owned by the British Museum—a sarcophagus that was itself a fake, though that fact would not be discovered for another twenty years. Marshall bought this second figure too, again through the dealer who acted as middleman.

In 1921, Fioravanti and the Riccardis turned out the large helmeted head. They used as their model a small terra-cotta head which, by a curious twist of fate, also ended up in the collection of the Metropolitan Museum. After that, apparently, Fioravanti went out of the business of producing fake Etruscan antiquities.

Parsons had Fioravanti write and sign a confession. He sent the document to James Rorimer, director of the Metropolitan Museum, in January, 1961.

The Metropolitan, meanwhile, had also been having some second thoughts about the three statues. While Parsons was interviewing Fioravanti, the Metropolitan's ceramics expert, Joseph V. Noble, had been carrying out an analysis of the pieces, with disturbing results. His tests showed that the "Greek black" glaze contained manganese dioxide, a coloring agent that had not been used before the nineteenth century.

Thus the arrival of Parsons' letter and Fioravanti's confession seemed to clinch the case against the statues. Director Rorimer hastily sent the current curator of classical art, Dietrich von Bothner, to Rome to talk to Fioravanti. Bothner and Fioravanti met at Parsons' apartment. Bothner had brought with him a plaster cast of one of the hands of the large warrior. The hand was missing a thumb.

169

Fioravanti had kept the thumb as a souvenir when he made the statue. He produced it now, and it fit the cast perfectly. Dietrich von Bothner sent word back to Rorimer in New York; there was no longer any possibility of doubt, he said. The thumb was the clincher. The sculptures were fakes, and Fioravanti was the man responsible. A few days later, the Metropolitan Museum issued its statement on the awkward discovery. The celebrated Etruscan statues would have to be written off as hoaxes. The only known monumental Etruscan sculpture had turned out to be fakes—though strikingly handsome ones.

The Metropolitan Museum of Art still has the three statues that caused so many red faces for its staff in 1961. The labels are different today, though. In place of the confident statement, "Etruscan—About 500 B.C.," the labels now read: "20th century Italian in the style of 5th century B.C. Etruscan." Alfredo Fioravanti gets no credit for them, but he probably does not mind. Whether or not his name is on the label, the old Italian craftsman has the pleasure of knowing that three products of his gifted hand are kept in the hallowed halls of the Metropolitan Museum of Art.

10: The Case of the
Venezuelan Ape-Man

The jungles and seas of the world hold many mysteries. Just before World War II, the sea off Madagascar yielded a live coelacanth, a weird fish thought to have been extinct for millions of years. Many explorers have spoken of glimpsing strange beasts in the steaming jungles of South America, animals otherwise unknown to zoology. From time to time, one of these travelers comes out of the jungle with a tale that sends the scientists into an uproar. François de Loys did just that in 1929 with his story of the Venezuelan ape-man. 171

De Loys was a Swiss oil geologist who had been exploring the Venezuelan wilderness between 1917 and 1920. While camped on the banks of the Catatumbo River in the Sierra de Perija forest, southeast of Lake Maracaibo, de Loys had an unexpected encounter with two strange creatures that suddenly emerged from the forest.

He thought at first that they were "a pair of red-haired men of the woods." As they drew closer, de Loys observed that one was male and one was female, and that they were not wild men at all, but very large apes of a kind he had never seen before. Both of them, de Loys said, "were very angry." They tore branches from the trees and hurled them at the startled geologist, scooped up handfuls of dirt and flung them at the men, and seemed about to launch an all-out attack.

There was no chance to capture either of them alive, so fierce and strong were they. De Loys quickly aimed his rifle and fired. "The female," he later wrote, "covered the male with her body and fell dead; the male then took to his heels and disappeared into the undergrowth of the jungle." Cautiously going forward, de Loys saw that the female ape was dead. He called the native members of his expedition over to look at it. None of them had ever seen anything like it: an ape almost five feet tall, covered with reddish hair, and much more human in appearance than any known monkey of the South American jungles.

172   De Loys knew that he had an important zoological

specimen, which should be brought back to civilization for further study. But he was on an oil-prospecting journey, not a zoological collecting expedition. He had no way to embalm or preserve the ape's body. It would be months or even years before he reached a city where the proper supplies could be procured for preparing the ape. In the tropical heat of the jungle, the body would decay and decompose in a matter of days.

De Loys did the best he could, under the circumstances. To afford a record of the creature's appearance while alive, he seated it on an oil can, propping it up with a long stick under its lower jaw, and took a photograph. Then he had the ape skinned, putting the hide in a box filled with salt in the hope that that would preserve it. He put the ape's skull in another box.

Then the expedition continued on its quest for oil. As de Loys' party came to the Tarra River region, a band of wild Motilones Indians swooped down. The geologists barely escaped with their lives. De Loys was wounded by an arrow. In the confusion, the skull and skin of the strange ape were lost. When de Loys finally reached civilization, months later, all he had was the photograph.

He showed it, some years afterward, to Georges Montandon, a French anthropologist. Montandon was excited by de Loys' story and questioned him closely. The geologist told Montandon that the ape had weighed about 112 pounds, been tailless, walked upright on its hind legs, and had thirty-two teeth, more human than apelike in form.

173

Montandon had nothing to go by except de Loys' story and the photograph. Nevertheless, he was convinced that de Loys had given an accurate description. Montandon coined a scientific name for the ape: *Ameranthropoides loysi,* "De Loys' man-like American ape." He published a scientific paper on it. Soon after, in June, 1929, de Loys himself told the world of his discovery in an article published in the *Illustrated London News,* a weekly magazine of good reputation that often ran popular science articles. De Loys' piece was accompanied by the photograph he had taken of the dead ape. The article was headed, "A Gap Filled in the Pedigree of Man."

And the scientific uproar began.

What was so important about the discovery of a large reddish ape in the Venezuelan jungles? Was the finding of a new sort of ape as significant as all that?

Yes, very much so, for no one had ever found any sort of ape in the Western Hemisphere—alive or fossilized. The creature de Loys claimed to have found, if accepted by science, would bring about a sweeping revolution in the theory of the evolution of man.

Man is a primate—a member of that order of mammals which has large brains, hands developed for grasping, teeth adapted for a mixed diet of flesh and vegetable foods, and certain other special characteristics. The order of primates includes some very primitive animals, such as the lemurs, tarsiers, and tree shrews, but its most

familiar representatives are the monkeys, the apes—
and ourselves.

The monkeys are divided into two groups, Old World
Monkeys and New World Monkeys. The New World
Monkeys are also called platyrrhine or "broad-nosed"
monkeys, because their noses are flat and the nostrils are
set wide apart. They have thirty-six teeth, and many of
them have prehensile tails, that is, their tails are practically a fifth arm, capable of curling around branches to
support the weight of the body. The platyrrhine monkeys
of South and Central America are generally small, some
of them—like the marmosets—hardly bigger than squir-
rels. There are some bigger ones, like the sapajous or
capuchin monkeys, the most advanced of the New
World Monkeys. Even they, however, do not have well-
developed hands. They are unable to oppose the thumb
and the fingers, which is necessary for any delicate ma-
nipulations, and they are tree-dwellers with prehensile
tails.

The Old World Monkeys are quite different, and
much more highly developed. They are known as catarrhine or "long-nosed" monkeys; their noses are narrow, the nostrils close together. They have thirty-two
teeth. Some of them, such as the baboons, the macaques,
and the mandrills, have tails, but not prehensile ones.
The catarrhine monkeys tend to be quite large, and often
quite intelligent.

The biggest and brightest of the catarrhine group are
the apes—the anthropoid, or "manlike" apes. These in- 175

clude the gibbon, the orangutan, the chimpanzee, and the gorilla. They have no tails, and they customarily walk on their hind legs, though supporting themselves by hooking their long arms in branches, or, in the case of the gorilla, by leaning forward to rest the knuckles against the ground. The anthropoid apes—particularly the chimpanzee—are the most intelligent of animals but for man himself. They can easily be taught, and they show many manlike traits of behavior, as anyone who has watched them in the zoo can testify. They are very much more intelligent than any of the New World Monkeys. As Thomas Henry Huxley, the earliest supporter of Charles Darwin's theory of evolution, said in 1860, "The difference between a New World Monkey and a chimpanzee is far greater than that between a chimpanzee and a man."

Human beings are not descended from the chimpanzees or the gorillas. But, according to modern evolutionary theory, mankind and the Old World Monkeys all have a common ancestor. Perhaps as long ago as ten or fifteen million years, there existed a simple, not overly intelligent tailless primate from whom all of today's apes and men are descended. As the years passed, millions of them, various families branched off from the "tree" of this original ancestor, and went their own evolutionary ways. One family evolved into the chimpanzees, another into the gorillas. Another lost most of its body hair, developed an upright posture, and became

176   ourselves.

The New World Monkeys don't fit into this evolutionary scheme at all. Those simpleminded chatterers, with their prehensile tails and their four extra teeth, must have branched away from the primate stock much earlier. They are only remotely related to us and do not lie on our path of evolutionary development.

So far as we know there never were any monkeys of the Old World type in the Western Hemisphere. The New World lived in complete isolation from the rest of the world during the millions of years that the higher apes and mankind were evolving from their unknown common ancestor. So man himself is an Old World product. Today's anthropologists believe that man's evolution took place in Africa and Asia. Gradually he moved northward into the colder parts of the globe. He did not reach North America until about thirty thousand years ago, when he had almost completely evolved into his modern form. Then, human beings crossed out of Asia via the Bering Strait, and fanned out over the Americas. As for the anthropoid apes, the gorillas, chimps, gibbons, and orangs, they never made the great migration into the Western Hemisphere. They stayed behind.

That theory is based on the fossil evidence. So far, no one has excavated the fossil bones of any anthropoid ape in the Americas. Nor has anyone found the remains of such primitive forms of man as Pithecanthropus or Neanderthal man. And, of course, no one has ever seen any live anthropoid apes in the Americas either, except for 177 the imported specimens in the zoos, and the one that François de Loys said he shot in the jungles of Venezuela.

There had been legends, though. The Mayan Indians of Yucatán had left two puzzling stone statues that seemed to portray manlike apes. A Mexican archaeological guidebook says of these statues, "They lack legs, but they are shown in an upright position and are about five feet tall. Their prominent eyebrow ridges, broad chests, and curved backs give them a strikingly apelike appearance: they look just like a pair of gorillas." Such nineteenth-century naturalists as Alexander von Humboldt and Philip Henry Gosse failed to find any anthropoid apes in South America, but they heard native tales of "wild men" and "hairy men," and agreed that it was quite possible that unknown apes might very well lurk in the unexplored recesses of the jungle.

While zoologists hunted in vain for some tailless ape that might upset the established theory, an Argentinian fossil hunter claimed better luck in the search for the bones of man's New World ancestors. He was Fiorino Ameghino of Buenos Aires, who began excavating in the Argentine pampas in 1873, when he was nineteen, and went on issuing strange and disturbing scientific statements for the next fifty years.

Ameghino's worst error as a scientist was to let himself be blinded by patriotism. He wanted to prove that man had originated in Argentina. He found a variety of fossil remains which he dated as far back as the Miocene

178

epoch, some fifteen million years ago. They were tiny but looked human to him, and he set them up as the ancestors of the New World Monkeys in one case, of the gibbons in another, and of man in the third.

Then he found more bones which he dated as Pliocene, say, two or three million years old. He gave these the name of Prothomo, "pre-man." That was in 1888. Eight years later, some bones found during construction work in Buenos Aires gave Ameghino the immediate ancestor of Prothomo: "half-man," Diprothomo. Supposedly, he flourished five or ten million years ago. Soon after, Ameghino turned up a Triprothomo who was even older, and then Tetraprothomo, man's earliest known ancestor, dating back some thirty million years.

Ameghino's wild ideas were couched in scientific terms. He issued elaborate descriptions of his finds, declaring, "This whole multiplicity of forms supports my supposition that man evolved from South American monkeys and that his primitive forerunners appeared in South America as long ago as the Mid Tertiary." He was no hoaxer, though, just the victim of his own delusions and ignorance. In 1912, a Swiss paleontologist named Bluntschli studied Ameghino's collection of bones and demolished most of the Argentinian's claims. Prothomo was the skull of a deformed but very recent Indian; so was Diprothomo. The earlier forms, in some cases, were not the bones of primates at all, but of "a tiny mammal, whose membership of any particular order cannot at present be established." Some of Ameghino's "fossil pri- 179 mates," Bluntschli found, were really the remains of small hoofed animals. Some of the primate skulls were genuine, but Ameghino had misinterpreted their importance. "They have no claim to the status of ancestral forms of the Old World monkeys," Bluntschli declared, but "they are nevertheless of the greatest importance to the history of the South American monkeys."

That disposed of Ameghino, and left the history of ancient man in the Americas exactly where it had been before: man was a latecomer, and the anthropoid apes had never been here at all.

Then, in 1929, along came François de Loys and his anthropoid ape from Venezuela to upset the whole situation all over again.

Georges Montandon, the anthropologist who had studied de Loys' claim, reviewed all the evidence for man-like apes in the Americas. He did not refer to Ameghino, who had been thoroughly discredited. He did mention the mysterious Mayan statues that looked "just like a pair of gorillas," and cited the conjectures of Humboldt, Philip Gosse, and other naturalists who were interested in the subject.

Late in 1929, the Paris Academy of Science met to discuss Montandon's paper. The members of the academy were not inclined to be friendly. When any new evidence is found that seems to explode a well-established theory, it is rarely received with delight. The scientists of the academy were very much in an "I'm from

Missouri" mood as they questioned Montandon about de Loys' anthropoid ape.

De Loys had said the ape was nearly five feet tall, a foot and a half taller than the sapajou, the biggest of the New World Monkeys. But this did not seem apparent from the photograph, Montandon was told.

He replied that the photo showed the ape sitting on a standard type of oil can. These oil cans, he said, were exactly eighteen inches high. The ape was three and a third times as tall as the can, according to the photograph—or five feet tall.

The professors grudgingly conceded that point. Perhaps the ape was so big, perhaps not. Much more important was the question of the tail. Tailless apes were unknown in South America. The entire significance of de Loys' find rested on the tailless nature of this ape. But the photograph showed a front view. It was impossible to tell whether the animal had had a tail or not. Certainly no tail was visible in the photograph.

"De Loys could have concealed the tail," one critic objected. "Or he could have amputated it altogether," said another.

Montandon tried to defend de Loys. Did the members of the Academy of Science seriously think, he asked, that the geologist would spend his time amputating the tail of a dead ape to make it look like a true anthropoid? If de Loys had removed the tail, surely he would have taken a rear-view photograph to make his case more convincing. Since he had not bothered to do so, he evidently expected that his word would not be questioned. The ape, said Montandon, had no tail.

The matter of the teeth was questioned. De Loys had said that the ape had had thirty-two teeth. The skull, alas, had been lost; there was no evidence but de Loys' statement. Now all New World Monkeys have thirty-six teeth, except for certain extremely small forms such as the marmoset and the midas monkey, which have thirty-two. Thirty-two teeth is a characteristic of the Old World Monkeys—and of man. Had de Loys possibly failed to count the wisdom teeth? De Loys was a geologist, not a dental expert, and if the mysterious ape were only a sapajou with small wisdom teeth, he might well have made a mistake. Or perhaps the wisdom teeth had not developed at all, as often happens in primates. No, the number of teeth alone did not prove that this was an Old World Monkey.

The critics of de Loys' ape turned next to the photograph itself. Didn't the animal look like a sapajou? It had the oddly curved thumb of the sapajou. It had the widely separated nostrils of a New World Monkey. It had the prehensile feet of a sapajou. In short, the opponents said, the animal in the picture was a sapajou. The only evidence to the contrary consisted of de Loys' claim that the animal had had no tail (not proven), that it had been five feet tall (likewise), and that it had had only thirty-two teeth (a minor point).

Montandon retreated under heavy fire. He admitted that the proofs all looked rather shaky, yet he continued to maintain that de Loys' animal was new and important. Montandon even said that he detected a definitely human appearance about the creature; its forehead was shaped, he said, like that of certain primitive forms of man. Montandon classified the Venezuelan creature as a hominid, or member of the human group, rather than as a pongid, a member of the group of great apes that includes the chimpanzee and the gorilla. "If the latter impression [of the shape of the forehead] is not an optical illusion due to the photograph," Montandon wrote, "then the possibility cannot be ruled out that the creature is an early hominid, a kind of parallel to *Pithecanthropus*."

Other scientists found a more conservative way of putting it. They thought that de Loys' Ameranthropoides might well be a highly developed New World Monkey, which, given a few million years of further evolution, might become something quite human, just as in the Old World evolutionary line the small-brained, chinless Pithecanthropus had given way in time to the modern *Homo sapiens*. Thus one French zoologist wrote, "The newly discovered animal is undoubtedly not connected to the Old World Monkeys, but is a typical New World Monkey—more accurately, a member of the sapajou family. But it seems to have attained a stage of evolution far in advance of all known monkeys of the New World."

Few anthropologists bought the idea that Ameranthropoides was any sort of apelike man or manlike ape. 183

"The photo shows a sapajou," they declared. "Possibly de Loys cut its tail off, or possibly he just hid it from sight." The matter ended right there. De Loys, having made his spectacular claim, refused to back it up with any further statements. He returned to the business of being a geologist, and Ameranthropoides never got into the zoological textbooks.

Was it a hoax?

Had de Loys cooked up the whole story, exaggerated the size of his ape, invented the notion that it was without a tail? We will never know. De Loys himself kept out of the limelight, and no one has any real insight into his motives. Perhaps he was having some fun with the anthropologists. Perhaps he simply made an error of observation. Or, perhaps, he actually did see and shoot an anthropoid ape in the jungles of Venezuela, and was the first and only man to bring back evidence that large manlike apes were native to the New World.

For years afterward, other travelers sought in vain to find de Loys' ape. A zoologist named Herschkowitz searched the Catatumbo River area intensively, found no Ameranthropoides alive or dead, and decided that de Loys must have been misled by some odd-looking sort of sapajou, possibly one that had lost its tail in a fight.

Then, in 1951, came a fresh report, published in the French paper *Candide*. Roger de Courteville, a mining engineer and explorer, declared that he had visited de Loys' ape-sighting territory several times, and had twice seen a red-haired manlike ape that walked on its hind legs, once in 1938 and again in 1947. Courteville had been the first man to cross South America by car, in 1926, and he had a considerable reputation as a traveler. When he produced a sketch of a live Ameranthropoides, quite clearly devoid of a tail, it caused as much of a stir as de Loys' original announcement more than twenty years before.

Courteville told of coming face-to-face with the ape. "Suddenly," he wrote, "a man-like creature was staring at me from a distance of only a few yards. It had a dull-witted expression: I thought at first it was an Indian of unknown race. The face was beardless, the skin dark; the gray-blue eyes beneath powerful ridges seemed perfectly gentle. A mop of red hair hung over its forehead, and the body and limbs were also covered in tufts of reddish hair. The creature's distinctly beast-like general appearance was in striking contrast to its peaceable disposition."

He was able to examine the ape in detail. His report told of the ape's receding chin, long arms and thighs, and deep chest. The ape not only posed for sketches, but also obliged Courteville by leaving footprints for him in fine sand, "footprints which showed me that, like the chimpanzee, it rested its weight on the outer edge of the foot."

The same year that Courteville had his first meeting with Ameranthropoides, he said, another traveler identified only as a Dr. de Barle had met one also, and had photographed it. Dr. de Barle's photo accompanied 185

Courteville's article. The animal in the photo did not much resemble the one in Courteville's sketches—his looked more like a gorilla, the photograph showed a sapajoulike animal—but Courteville insisted that they were one and the same.

Courteville's fondness for details did him in. Zoologists pointed out that known New World Monkeys, as well as the Ameranthropoides of de Loys' original photograph, walk on the whole sole of the foot, not on the outer edge. Courteville had misread his own evidence.

Then, too, the gorillalike face of Courteville's sketches did not resemble, by any stretch of the imagination, the photo taken by Dr. de Barle. As for Dr. de Barle, who was he and where was he? No one else had heard of him.

Worst of all was the photograph itself. A close look showed that it was simply a doctored copy of de Loys' old picture. Someone had edited out the stick that propped up the dead ape, had covered up the oil can, and had painted in a jungle backdrop. The ape was the same.

Possibly Courteville was the victim of someone who sold him the fraudulent photo, but he went on claiming that he really had seen the manlike ape. His statements seem like such an obvious hoax that they have cast discredit backward on de Loys. Now he, too, seems like nothing more than a hoaxer.

186   Is he? Does his photograph show merely a dead sapa-

jou? Or did he actually see a large tailless anthropoid ape on the banks of the Catatumbo River?

Nobody knows. The case of the Venezuelan ape-man remains unsolved. Until further evidence turns up—real evidence—the mysterious ape of François de Loys and Roger de Courteville must remain in the realm of phantoms.

11: The Kammerer
Tragedy

P aul Kammerer reached the end
of the line in September, 1926. The brilliant Austrian
biologist, who had been hailed as "the modern Darwin"
and as the man who "has made perhaps the greatest
biological discovery of the century," walked into the
Theresien hills near the Austrian village of Puchberg
and sent a bullet through his brain. He was forty-six
years old, and his death was the climax of an audacious
and impudent scientific hoax, for which Paul Kammerer
188 was responsible.

Or was Kammerer the victim of a hoaxer himself? Perhaps. Whatever the truth, there is no denying that his story is one of science's most tragic.

Kammerer had been something of a lone wolf in biology. He believed in a theory of evolution, but not Darwin's theory. Kammerer went back to an earlier concept, put forth by the French naturalist Jean Baptiste Lamarck.

Lamarck, who was born in 1744 and died in 1829, taught that acquired characteristics could be inherited. That is to say, changes wrought in a person's lifetime could be transmitted to his children at their birth. The children of a blacksmith, who stands all day hammering at his anvil, would be born with unusually powerful arms. The children of a pianist, who practices his scales six hours a day, would have nimble, agile fingers. Lamarck explained all the special characteristics of animals this way.

Consider the long-legged birds, the cranes and herons and flamingos. Why are they built the way they are? Because, Lamarck said, they "wish" to wade through the water in search of food without getting their bodies wet. So their legs grow longer and longer, and their offspring inherit these long legs. Or, Lamarck said, take the giraffe with his long neck. He feeds by nibbling leaves from trees. Once he has eaten all the leaves on the lower branches, he must reach ever higher, or starve. Generation after generation of such neck-stretching gave the giraffe a permanently long neck; baby giraffes were   189 born long-necked. In the same way, Lamarck explained the webbed feet of ducks, the thick fur of animals living in cold climates, and all other characteristics of living things. A need arises, said Lamarck, and the animal changes in response to the need—and these changes are inherited by future generations.

Lamarck's theory was actually an important one in its day. He lived at a time when scientists were reluctant to believe that species could change at all. They held that God had created all the different kinds of animals and plants at the beginning of time, and that it was impossible for any living thing to change its form. Lamarck collected a great deal of proof to show that species did evolve, but his ideas about the way evolution happens were much too simpleminded. Blacksmiths do not always have muscular children. Giraffes do not pass long necks to their offspring simply by "wishing" to reach high branches.

In the middle of the nineteenth century, England's Charles Darwin put Lamarck's theory on a more scientific footing. Darwin suggested the idea of "natural selection" to explain the changes in a living thing's form. His chief point was that certain changes tended to increase an organism's chance of survival. These changes were handed to succeeding generations simply because organisms which did not have the new trait were less likely to live long enough to have offspring.

In the case of giraffes, Darwin's theory suggested that
190 originally giraffes might well have been short-necked

creatures that had to strain and stretch to reach the higher branches. But, strain all they wished, they could not extend the length of their children's necks by a fraction of an inch. Then, the new theory said, a few giraffes with slightly longer necks might have been born. Darwin did not explain *why* this might happen. It simply happened.

The taller giraffes could reach the upper branches. They ate more, became strong and healthy, lived longer, and had more offspring. The offspring of long-necked giraffes tended to have longer necks themselves. Meanwhile, the short-necked giraffes were hard put to find food. They could not equal the competition. Many of them died of starvation without having any offspring at all; others had just a few. Gradually, the long-necked giraffes came to outnumber the original kind, because they were better equipped for survival. The short-necked giraffes dwindled and disappeared over the course of generations.

Darwin had said that such changes as the development of long necks in giraffes came about "by chance," meaning "from an unknown cause." Not until some years after his death was the reason for the changes made clear. The theory of mutations (changes) was worked out at the beginning of the present century. According to this way of thinking, mutations occur at random all the time among living things. The inherited characteristics of an organism are controlled by microscopic bodies known as chromosomes, which are found within the cells that cause reproduction. The chromosomes, in turn, contain even smaller bodies called genes that carry the specific characteristics. Among humans, for example, there is a gene for skin color, one for blue eyes, one for freckles, and one for long legs. Our appearance is determined by the mixture of genes that we receive from our parents.

These genes can be altered in various ways. Some of the mutations that result from spontaneous changes in the genes are so tiny they are hardly noticeable. Others are more conspicuous. Sometimes babies are born with six fingers, for example. Some mutations are so harmful that the child cannot survive: a baby born with its heart outside the body, say.

In the case of most really radical mutations, the mutant dies in infancy, or is unable to reproduce. So the mutated characteristic is lost. But some mutations are useful, because they help the individual to survive. The mutation that gave the giraffe a longer neck was such a positive evolutionary development. So was the mutation that put fur on the polar bear and the mutation that enabled the green frog to camouflage itself against a green leaf. These were useful mutations, beneficial to the organism, and so, having popped up in a random way, they endured through a process of Darwinian natural selection.

This is a neat, logical theory, and nearly all scientists had accepted it by about 1920. The old Lamarckian notions about animals changing through constant neck-stretching had given way to this much more reasonable concept. Experiments had shown that Lamarck's ideas simply did not work. Late in the nineteenth century, the German biologist August Weismann had destroyed Lamarck's theories by cutting the tails off 1,592 mice. Weismann had lopped the tails off a few mice and then had allowed them to breed. The baby mice were born with tails. Weismann cut their tails off. They grew up and produced offspring who had tails, of which they were deprived in short order. On and on went the experiment, through twenty-two generations of mice. Weismann finally concluded that he could cut the tails from his mice till doomsday without bringing about the birth of a single tailless mouse. So much for the theory of the inheritance of acquired characteristics!

But there were some men who shrugged off Darwin, Weismann, and the rest of modern science, and clung to Lamarck. They had philosophical reasons for wanting to believe that the wish to change was enough to bring about a permanent change. Darwin, they said, left no room for free will and individual effort. Was it not possible to improve through striving? Did all progress come about in a random way, through chance mutations? That seemed degrading and negative. These men preferred to believe that a man's efforts to improve himself would show directly in his offspring, so that each new generation would display greater progress toward perfection.

One man who felt this way was Paul Kammerer. His   193

book, *The Inheritance of Acquired Characteristics*, published in 1924, declared, "If acquired characteristics cannot be passed on . . . then no true organic progress is possible. Man lives and suffers in vain. Whatever he might have acquired in the course of a lifetime dies with him. His children and his children's children must ever and again start from the bottom."

On the other hand, Kammerer wrote, "If acquired characteristics are occasionally inherited, then it becomes evident that we are not exclusively slaves of the past—slaves helplessly endeavoring to free ourselves of our shackles—but also captains of our future, who in the course of time will be able to rid ourselves, to a certain extent, of our heavy burdens and to ascend into higher and ever higher strata of development."

Noble words. And Kammerer thought he had the scientific proof to back the theory soundly with facts.

Kammerer, born in Vienna in 1880, was a tireless researcher, a man of great energy and keen intelligence. He was a sensitive human being, too, refusing to perform any experiments that might cause pain to any living creature. He kept his experimental animals in specially designed laboratories as much like their natural environment as possible. Politically, also, Kammerer was conscious of the sufferings of others; he was a dedicated socialist, spending much of his time assisting the poverty-stricken and homeless.

194   He was associated with the Institute for Experimental

Biology of the University of Vienna. The institute, strangely, had its headquarters in the Prater, Vienna's amusement park. In a building that once had been a public aquarium, Kammerer passed long hours in the dank, dark, cold basement, where he carried out observations on olms, large European salamanders that normally live in flooded caves.

Kammerer began to study olms in 1903. He began with forty of them. Olms are slow to reproduce, but young ones were born late in 1905, more in 1906, still more a year later. And Kammerer noticed some odd things about these baby olms.

Living in the darkness of caves, olms in the natural state are blind. Their eyes are covered by membranes of skin. They are pale-colored creatures, like most cave animals. But Kammerer found that adult olms, when exposed to light in his laboratory, tended to turn darker. The baby olms also darkened when exposed to light. One baby olm in particular began to develop fully formed eyes, which gradually bulged through the membrane of skin by the time the salamander was five years old. Normally, olms were born with eyes, but, having no use in pitch darkness, the eyes never developed.

Kammerer might perhaps have tried to breed a species of olms with eyes, by exposing baby olms to light and mating them. Instead, he concentrated on the other important effect—the darkening of the skin. By raising his olms in an illuminated aquarium, he caused their skins to turn dark—in much the same way that suntan

195

will darken the skin of a human being. Kammerer put his adult, darkened olms back into darkness to let them mate. The children were born with dark skins!

He immediately argued that here was a case of the inheritance of acquired characteristics. He had exposed olms to light; their skins had turned dark; they had given birth to dark offspring! What could be a clearer example of Lamarck's theory?

His fellow biologists did not agree. Weismann, he of the mouse-tail experiment, pointed out that the olm's skin is transparent in the normal state. Light passing through the skin of the salamanders might well have reached the germ cells, those which house the chromosomes and genes. Light striking the genes could have caused a mutation leading to dark-skinned offspring. So Kammerer's results could be explained in terms of orthodox genetic theory.

There was no way for Kammerer to defeat such an argument—except by using some other experimental animal, one that did not have a transparent skin and so might not be as susceptible to mutation. He chose two new subjects: the fire salamander and the midwife toad.

The fire salamander is a common European amphibian, a plump creature four or five inches long. Its skin is deep black in color, with large, shiny yellow spots. Kammerer felt that the color of the fire salamander could be influenced by its environment. He said that it would tend to change its color to make itself less conspicuous, thereby concealing itself from its natural enemies.

He raised one family of fire salamanders in a terrarium whose top soil was a deep, lustrous black hue. He raised another set of salamanders on soil of a yellowish cast. He reported that the salamanders raised on black soil were gradually losing their yellow spots. Each new generation of salamanders had smaller spots than the last. Over in the other terrarium, the opposite was happening. The salamanders on yellowish soil were developing bigger and bigger yellow spots—so that before long they would seem entirely yellow!

It was a stunning development. The biologists of Europe and America read Kammerer's reports in disbelief and confusion. Was it possible that he could breed all-black salamanders and all-yellow salamanders simply by raising black-and-yellow ones against backdrops of solid yellow or solid black? That went counter to every development in genetics since Darwin's day. Yet Kammerer belonged to the much-respected Institute for Experimental Biology, and his statements had to be taken seriously.

Even more startling were his accomplishments with the midwife toad. The mating of most toads takes place in water, and the male toad has a special adaptation that allows him to hold the slippery female still during the mating act: pads like small warts on the front feet, known as "nuptial pads."

The midwife toad, however, mates on land, where it is less of a problem to maintain contact between male and female. The male midwife toad therefore does not need

197

or have nuptial pads. He plays a curious part in the hatching of the eggs, by the way. After the female has laid the eggs, the male midwife toad wraps them in long loops around his hind legs. Then he digs a hole in moist sand or earth, and squats there for several weeks while the eggs mature. When they are just about ready to hatch, he heads for water. The eggs hatch in water and the tadpoles develop normally from that point on, coming up on land when they are old enough to mate.

Kammerer wondered what would happen if midwife toads were forced to stay in water all their lives. Simply keeping them in an aquarium without any dry area struck him as too drastic a change, so he built a terrarium that had both land and water. But he kept the temperature at 90° F.—too hot for a toad's comfort. The toads spent most of their time in the water, and when it was mating time they mated in the water, as other species do. Before long, Kammerer's toads developed the habit of mating in water, so that when he returned a pair of toads to a cooler terrarium where they could mate on land, they went on using the water anyway.

Furthermore, he said, the tadpoles produced by these water matings grew up into toads who also preferred to mate in water. Even when he permitted these young toads to hatch in what was for them a normal environment, they followed the pattern of their parents, and mated in water.

Most spectacular of all was Kammerer's report that at 198 least one of his male toads had acquired a new physical characteristic as a result of the water matings. He had developed nuptial pads! His forefeet showed the little wartlike protuberances that were common to water-mating toads!

The news caused a worldwide scientific sensation, as might be expected. An enthusiastic English scientist, Dr. Thornley Garden, professor of zoology at Cambridge, declared, "Kammerer begins where Darwin left off." It was another Cambridge man, the biologist G. H. F. Nuttall, who unwisely offered the opinion that "He has made perhaps the greatest biological discovery of the century."

Kammerer also attracted favorable attention in Russia. Russia had a disciple of Lamarck too—Ivan Vladimirovich Michurin, who since 1880 had been carrying out agricultural experiments. Michurin had raised fruit, vegetables, and corn that were remarkably well adapted to the harsh climatic conditions of central Russia. He had little or no knowledge of the theory of genetics, but claimed that his undeniably excellent results came from making changes in the environment of his plants. He had, he said, brought about the inheritance of acquired characteristics.

When Communism came to power in Russia in 1917, Michurin was hailed as a national hero. The official Communist belief concerning evolution was that Lamarck had been right and Darwin and his followers wrong. According to the party line, man is a product of his environment, and can be altered by altering that environment. The Communists extended this to science; they found it necessary to argue that what they believed was true of society was also true of nature. So when Kammerer came along with what looked like experimental proof that Lamarck and Michurin were correct, he became a Soviet hero.

Michurin was then a very old man. The Russians badly needed someone to replace him as a professor at the University of Moscow. Kammerer seemed ideal. He was a Westerner, who could bring the latest in scientific techniques to Russia, then a very backward and underdeveloped country. He was a socialist, so his politics were acceptable. Above all, he had the right ideas about Lamarck and evolution. A feeler went out to Kammerer in Vienna: was he interested in coming to Moscow as a professor?

Yes, Kammerer said. Gladly, but not just yet. First he had to convince his Western colleagues that his experiments were legitimate.

His book, *The Inheritance of Acquired Characteristics*, had stirred up controversy when it appeared in 1924. Most biologists and geneticists refused to believe Kammerer's results. "His work has not carried conviction to biologists as a whole, and in particular to those who ought to be best qualified to judge," wrote the biologist Julian Huxley in a review of the book. "It is a sad thing," Huxley added, "when a man has spent half a lifetime on researches which his colleagues will not accept."

Kammerer had first announced his astonishing results with salamanders and midwife toads in 1919. But in the years that followed he stubbornly refused to turn his specimens over to other scientists for examination. Finally, in 1926, Kammerer yielded. He agreed to allow a committee of his colleagues to look at his work.

The committee was headed by Dr. G. Kingsley Noble of the American Museum of Natural History in New York. Another investigator was Dr. Hans Przibram of the University of Vienna, the director of the institute where Kammerer had done his research. They visited Kammerer's laboratory, and he showed them the midwife toad that had grown the nuptial pads—dead, now, and preserved in a jar of alcohol. They looked at his other toads. They looked at his salamanders. Then, rather coolly, they took their leave.

A few weeks later, on August 7, 1926, the English scientific magazine *Nature* published two separate reports on Kammerer, one by Noble and one by Przibram. Both agreed that Kammerer's results were fraudulent. Noble had examined the so-called nuptial pads of the midwife toad and found that they were smooth, without the skin spines that should have been there. The black spots that marked the pads were below the skin, not in it. They were, in fact, nothing but spots of india ink that had been injected into the forefeet of the toad! When Noble dipped the toad's feet in water, the "nuptial pads" washed away.

Scientists throughout the world were aghast. They had

followed Kammerer's work with considerable bewilderment, but it was almost beyond belief that he could have tried to bring off such an amateurish hoax. How could it be? Was it possible?

There was consternation at the University of Vienna, too. Kammerer's immediate associates looked at him coldly and asked for an explanation. Kammerer stammered that he was not guilty, that he had not looked at the cases in months, that he could not imagine who had tampered with his specimens. Only two other men had keys to Kammerer's laboratory. One was Dr. Przibram, Kammerer's director and close friend. The other was a biologist named Megusar, who had disliked Kammerer and often had quarreled with him. Had Megusar altered Kammerer's specimens? No one could answer, for Megusar had died several months before.

For six weeks, Kammerer lived a shadowy life, speaking to no one, his laboratory shrouded in gloom and despair. On September 22, 1926, he wrote a long, rambling letter to the Moscow Academy of Science, heading it, "Respected Comrades and Colleagues." He said that he had read the "attack upon me made by Dr. Noble in *Nature*," and had gone to examine his specimens himself. "I found the statements of Dr. Noble completely verified," Kammerer declared. In fact, not only had the midwife toad been artificially endowed with india-ink nuptial pads, but a "black" salamander turned out to have had its yellow spots covered up by ink as well.

Kammerer told the Russians that he had no idea who

might have perpetrated such a fraud. "There is no doubt, however," he wrote, "that thereby almost my whole life work has become dubious. Consequently, although I did not participate in this fraud, I feel that I am not entitled any more to accept your nomination. Moreover, I find it is impossible to survive the destruction of my life work. I hope to find tomorrow sufficient courage and fortitude to end my wretched life."

The next day, Kammerer died by his own hand.

The theory of acquired characteristics died with him in the Western world. Nothing could have more thoroughly shattered the Lamarckian idea than the bullet that took Paul Kammerer's life. With his toads and salamanders seen now as the products of a hoax, no one could take Kammerer's theories seriously any more.

Except in Russia. The comrades mourned Kammerer as a martyr of science. A Russian film was produced with Kammerer as its hero; the faking of the specimens was shown as the work of a scheming bishop and a capitalistic-minded member of the German royal family, then in exile. In this fictionalized version of the story, the fraud was discovered in time to forestall the hero's suicide, and the professor left the wicked West and traveled in triumph to Russia, the land of liberty, where such dastardly deeds were impossible.

The Russians were deadly serious about their evolutionary theory. In 1933, four Russian geneticists were sent to labor camps in Siberia for teaching a theory contrary to Lamarck's. Three years later, a geneticist named

203

Agol was put to death for his refusal to accept the official Communist line on evolution. Other important Russian scientists disappeared in 1938 during the campaign of terror ordered by the Russian dictator Stalin. Their crime, too, seems to have been believing in the modern theory of genes and chromosomes.

Heeding the fate of these men, the surviving Russian geneticists quickly abandoned their "capitalistic ideas," and followed the teaching of Stalin's favorite, Trofim Lysenko. Lysenko claimed to base his work on that of Michurin and Kammerer, and he rose to prominence in Russia with his assertions that Russian agriculture could be improved through careful use of Lamarckian methods.

After Stalin's death in 1953, Lysenko fell from popularity. His methods were not producing results where they counted—in the food supply. Nikita Khrushchev attacked Lysenko during the general denunciation of Stalin, calling the geneticist a "scientific monopolist" and an "academic schemer." By 1956, Lysenko was forced to resign his various scientific posts, and he dropped into obscurity. For the first time since 1917, it was possible for Russian geneticists to study some of the work being done in other countries where politics is not allowed to control science.

The mystery of the Kammerer hoax still remains unsolved. Did Kammerer tamper with the toads and salamanders himself? Was it done by one of his assistants, eager to produce the evidence Kammerer was looking for? Or was it the spiteful and mischievous work of some enemy of Kammerer's? Or was there some other, unknown, cause?

Kammerer's suicide does not automatically brand him as the guilty party. It could have been that he felt too disgraced and humiliated to go on living, even though innocent—for the exposure labeled him as a careless researcher, if not necessarily a fraud. Many charitable scientists feel that he was not actually responsible for the hoax. But, as Dr. Conway Zirkle wrote in his study of Lysenkoism, *Death of a Science in Russia*, we cannot excuse Kammerer from guilt until we can "explain Kammerer's seven-year reluctance to have his specimen examined, and his prolonged and skilful evasions of his critics' demands."

Professor Richard B. Goldschmidt, a scientist who knew Kammerer personally, also feels that he was the hoaxer. In an article published in *Science* in 1949, Dr. Goldschmidt wrote, "I do not believe that Kammerer was an intentional forger. He was a very high-strung, decadent but brilliant man who spent his nights, after a day in the laboratory, composing symphonies. . . . He conceived the idea that he could prove the inheritance of acquired characters and became so obsessed with this idea that he 'improved' upon his records. I have reason to believe, from what I have seen in his laboratory, that he continued his experiments, which ended by the death of the specimens, by starting again with similar-looking animals. . . . [He] did not consider this wrong. He

205

simply did not know what an experiment amounted to. In later years he probably became so absorbed with the necessity of proving his claims that he started inventing results or 'doctoring' them. Though the actual results of all this amounted to falsification, I am not certain that he realized it and intended it. He probably was a nervous wreck in the end."

Kammerer called himself a scientist and spoke and wrote like a scientist. But actually what he was doing was the opposite of true science. The scientist begins by observing facts, and eventually draws a theory from his observations. Kammerer began with a theory—Lamarck's—and twisted the facts to fit his ideas.

Wishful thinking is not science. Giraffes did not get their long necks by wishing, and Kammerer could not grow nuptial pads on midwife toads that way either. So he produced the pads himself, perhaps not even realizing, at that point, that he had ceased to be honest with his work or with himself. That was Paul Kammerer's true tragedy. The gunshot in the Theresien hills ended a life that had long since strayed from its proper path.

12: *Otto Fischer's Rocket Ride*

The first human being to take a rocket ride through space was a Russian cosmonaut, Major Yuri Alekseyevich Gagarin. On April 12, 1961, Major Gagarin clambered into a capsule mounted on a Soviet rocket and was blasted into an orbit that took him on a 108-minute ride around the earth. Shortly after, on May 5, 1961, American astronaut Commander Alan B. Shepard, Jr., boarded a Project Mercury capsule and was boosted into space by a Redstone rocket for a 15-minute suborbital space trip.

207

They are the pioneers of space travel. That is, unless we include a German named Otto Fischer, who took a trip through space in 1933—the year before Yuri Gagarin was born.

Space flight, in 1933, was something strictly out of science fiction. Government rocket research was unknown. The only rocket men were private experimenters, many of them isolated cranks and crackpots who frequently lost fingers or limbs in their quest to reach the moon. The test rockets they worked with were flimsy, unreliable things—mere toys by today's standards—that usually blew up before they got far off the ground. At best, their rockets rose a few thousand feet, which still left them better than 238,000 miles short of the moon. The total budget of the federal government in that Depression year of 1933 was $4,598,000,000, and an easy way to get branded as a madman would have been to predict that in another thirty years the United States would be spending more than that each year on space research alone.

That was the background against which this news article appeared, on November 5, 1933. It was a front-page item in the London *Sunday Referee:*

"History's first successful passenger rocket flight was achieved on October 29 on the Island of Rügen in the Baltic Sea, according to a special dispatch from Rügen. A sensational secret demonstration of the practicability of the rocket principle applied to flight was made there
208   last Sunday, when Herr Otto Fischer was shot 6 miles

into the air within a 24-foot steel rocket and returned to Earth safe and sound, though shaken.

"The pilot who risked his life in this experiment is a brother of the designer and constructor of the rocket, Herr Bruno Fischer. Owing to the disastrous result of a similar experiment made on Rügen in the spring of last year, when the original inventor was killed, the demonstration was made under the cover of absolute secrecy, under the auspices of the Reichswehr, the German War Ministry. The inhabitants of the island knew nothing of the proposed experiment and no members of the Press were called in to witness it. . . .

"On Sunday morning at 6 o'clock, Otto Fischer shook hands with his brother and the small group of Reichswehr officials present to witness the experiment and crawled through the small steel door. . . . There was a blinding flash and a deafening explosion and the slim torpedo-shaped body was gone from the steel framework in which it had rested. A few minutes later it came into sight again, floating nose upwards from a large parachute that had automatically been released when it had begun to descend. . . . A few seconds later it came to rest on the sands a few yards away and Fischer crawled through the door of the rocket, white and shaken, but smiling triumphantly. The journey through space had lasted 10 minutes and 26 seconds.

" 'It was a tremendous sensation,' he said. . . . 'I lost consciousness for a moment, due to the tremendous acceleration which drained the blood from my head. 209

When I came to my senses and looked at the altimeter before my face it flickered at 32,000 feet—a fraction over six miles—and then began to drop rapidly. I had completed my climb and was descending. . . . The next thing that occupied my attention was the tremendous heat of the asbestos floor on which I was standing. The reason was that the rocket had merely been propelled about two hundred feet by the initial explosion and had been driven the remainder of the distance by the rockets in its tail, which had been released automatically at timed intervals. . . .' "

It all sounds very much like a primitive version of the space flights that have become so familiar today. All the main features are there: the countdown at dawn, the final handshake, the blast-off, the astronaut's sensations as acceleration hits him, the parachute opening to ease the descent, and finally the first-hand report from the returned astronaut. When the *Sunday Referee*'s story appeared, space flight was still a strange and bizarre subject for most people. Newspapers in France, Switzerland, Germany, and Italy picked up the story and reprinted it. It found its way across the Atlantic to Boston, where a newspaper ran a condensed version of the story. The Boston article, in turn, was reprinted in the March, 1934, issue of *Wonder Stories*, one of the pioneering science-fiction magazines.

Wonder Stories was where the item belonged. The 1933 rocket fight was pure fiction, a work of fantasy from beginning to end. Those intrepid rocket experi-

210

menters, the brothers Bruno and Otto Fischer, did not exist. There had been no manned rocket flight in Germany or anywhere else. The lovely Baltic island of Rügen, with its white chalk cliffs and handsome forests, was a well-known vacation resort, but it did not have a rocket testing ground. The story was a hoax.

But it did not seem like a hoax to the public. Many people knew that the Germans had been engaged in serious rocket research for a number of years. It was quite possible that they might have achieved such a flight—so the laymen thought. There had been some publicity, too, for the American Rocket Society and its experiments, and for Dr. Robert H. Goddard, an obstinate experimenter who insisted on designing rockets despite total lack of support for his work. Rocketry was in the air that year. The Otto Fischer story had a tone of plausibility about it.

Those who were really active in rocket research, though, were immediately suspicious. They knew that a man-carrying rocket would have to weigh several thousand pounds, at the least. Most of the rockets then being built weighed less than a hundred pounds. No one knew more clearly than the rocket men themselves how thoroughly impossible the Fischer story was, in the year 1933. They wanted to believe the story, with all their hearts, for if it were true it would mean that a great advance in rocketry had been made. But they knew it could only be a hoax.

One of the experts most troubled by the Otto Fischer

story was a German rocket experimenter named Willy Ley. Though he was not quite thirty years old, Ley had been an important figure in German rocket research for nearly ten years. At the time the Fischer story saw print, Ley was quietly making plans to escape from Germany to avoid the persecutions of the new Nazi government. Indeed, soon after, he made his way to safety and began a new career as a science writer and lecturer in the United States.

Before he left, he checked up on the supposed manned rocket flight. Ley's verdict was that the story was a complete fabrication.

At that time, most rocket research in Germany was being carried on by a group called the Verein für Raumschiffahrt, or Society for Space Travel. Germans referred to it as the VfR, but it was commonly known in the English-speaking world as the German Rocket Society. It had been organized in 1927 by a handful of men in the small German town of Breslau, and among its earliest members were such German rocket men as Hermann Oberth, Max Valier, and Walter Hohmann, who played important roles in rocketry's early development. Within a year, the German Rocket Society had over five hundred members in many countries. Its roster included nearly everyone who had a deep interest in helping mankind reach other worlds—not a very great number back then, when even the airplane was still a novelty and space travel a wild dream.

212   In its first few years, the German Rocket Society con-

centrated mainly on publishing technical journals and booklets. It did not have the funds for actual experiments, though by September, 1929, its membership roll had risen to 870. Some of the members led a campaign to begin real rocket work, and funds were raised to test a small liquid-fuel rocket, a tiny ancestor of today's mighty missiles.

Robert Goddard had already tested a liquid-fuel rocket in Massachusetts in 1926; it had traveled 184 feet in two and a half seconds, attaining a speed of about sixty miles an hour. But the German Rocket Society had no information about Goddard's rocket. On July 23, 1930, it tested its own rocket, which "performed without mishap . . . for 90 seconds." Among the men taking part in the experiment was a young student named Wernher von Braun, today a leader in American space research.

A few months before that test, German rocketry had been marred by a tragedy: the death of rocketeer Max Valier, who had been conducting experiments with a rocket-powered automobile. Early in May, Valier was killed when the motor of his car exploded during a test run. His death would eventually play a part in the Otto Fischer rocket hoax.

During the summer of 1930, the German Rocket Society conducted further experiments with its small rocket, and later that year obtained its own testing ground—a tract of unused land two square miles in area, in a northern suburb of Berlin. The rocket men rented the land   213 from its owner, the city of Berlin, for a token fee, and beginning that September went into rocket research in earnest.

As finances allowed, the work went on. The German government refused to grant any money for the research —what good were rockets, anyway—and the various universities and scientific bodies also declined to help out. The first rocket had blown up in 1930; they built a second, slightly larger, and tested it a few times before it, too, blew up in the spring of 1931. Meanwhile, another German rocketry group managed to launch a liquid-fuel rocket weighing eleven pounds, on February 21, 1931. It rose only ten feet. A second test a month later was a little more successful, but rocketry in Germany was still a long way from the stage of manned rockets. The Berlin group was jubilant when one of its rockets traveled a mere two thousand feet in May, 1931.

Two years went by. The small, sputtering rockets failed to achieve any great success. Hitler came to power in Germany; the German Army began to get interested in rockets as weapons of war, and hired a few rocketry men, including Wernher von Braun. (A decade later, von Braun's V-2 rockets would terrorize Great Britain in World War II.)

In October, 1933—the month of the great German rocket flight of Otto Fischer—there was a second rocket tragedy in Germany. Reinhold Tiling, an engineer who was doing private rocket research with the backing of a wealthy industrialist, was killed in an explosion of his

214

laboratory. Tiling had been working on a rocket that he hoped would be capable of crossing the English Channel. He had had only scorn for the puny accomplishments of the German Rocket Society.

Tiling was killed on October 11. Eighteen days later, Otto Fischer supposedly made his historic rocket flight, and a week after that the *Sunday Referee* printed the story. The headquarters of the German Rocket Society was deluged with inquiries from everywhere. Had it really happened? Was it true? Who was Otto Fischer? More details were wanted.

Willy Ley set out to check the story.

He began by looking through the files of the German Rocket Society. There was no member named Otto Fischer, none named Bruno Fischer. In fact, there were no Fischers at all—a bit strange, he thought, since Fischer is a fairly common German name. Presumably anyone interested in rocketry would be a member of Europe's largest rocket society, Ley thought. The absence of Otto Fischer's name from the files was suspicious.

He turned next to the editor of the London *Sunday Referee*. The paper had credited the story to its "Special Correspondent, Rügen." That seemed fishy to Ley, for Rügen, that quiet seashore resort, was not important enough a news center to rate the presence of a special correspondent from an English newspaper. Not even the large German papers bothered to keep correspondents there.

215

The *Referee*'s editor, when pressed for information, told Ley that the story had been "accidentally obtained from a thoroughly reliable source." He would offer no further details. The vague reply was hardly encouraging.

Further checking failed to produce anyone connected with rocket research anywhere who had heard of the Fischer brothers. Ley picked up a rumor that Ernest Loebell of the Cleveland Rocket Society had checked the Fischer story and had found it to be correct. Off went a letter from Ley to Loebell; back came the reply that Loebell "had never bothered even thinking about so silly a story."

The text of the newspaper story itself struck Ley as a tissue of inconsistencies and errors. As he wrote later, "The steel construction of the rocket is a dubious point. All the rockets I know of were built wholly or at least partly of aluminum and aluminum alloys, and since the strength of the light alloys is sufficient there certainly is no need to substitute steel. That 'Otto Fischer' should have spoken of an altimeter needle quivering around 32,000 feet is a severe mistake on the part of the 'special correspondent.' Meters of all kinds built anywhere in Europe (if not England) are calibrated in meters and kilometers."

Ley was also troubled by the article's reference to an "asbestos floor" in the passenger compartment. The materials generally used for rocket insulation in Germany at that time were glass-wool or slag-wool, not asbestos. And Ley found the description of the rocket's climb "pure fantasy." The article had spoken of a number of separate rocket explosions propelling the vessel—whereas a real rocket would have had a single continuous engine thrust during the ascent.

The *Sunday Referee* quietly let the Fischer story slip into oblivion. Ley had shown conclusively that it had been a hoax. He demonstrated that the raw material for the story had come from actual events, though. Setting the flight in Germany was convincing, for Germany was known to be a leader in rocket research. Mentioning the "similar experiment" of the previous year, with its "disastrous result," the article led the readers to think that Max Valier's much-publicized death was meant. (Probably the author of the hoax was inspired in part by Reinhold Tiling's death a few weeks before publication of the article.)

There had even been a serious plan to make a manned rocket flight in the spring of 1933. An engineer named Mengering, who lived in the city of Magdeburg, a hundred miles from Berlin, had persuaded the officials of that city to sponsor a rocket experiment. Mengering had the wild idea that we live, not on the outer skin of a planet, but inside a huge hollow globe. He felt that a rocket rising skyward would crash into the "wall" that surrounded us.

The city fathers of Magdeburg had no interest in Mengering's geographical theories, but they were attracted by the publicity aspects of the attempt. They called in Rudolph Nebel, a rocket builder who had been associated with the German Rocket Society, and asked him to design a man-carrying rocket that could be fired in June, 1933, during a city festival. The rocket, as Nebel designed it, would be about twenty-five feet high, and its engine would generate some thirteen hundred pounds of thrust. Thus it would be vastly bigger than any rocket that had yet been constructed. At an altitude of thirty-three hundred feet, the passenger was to be ejected from his compartment, and would parachute to earth.

Nebel began by building smaller rockets as models. Some fairly big rockets, weighing up to two hundred and fifty pounds, were tested with uneven results. By June 9, 1933, Nebel was ready to launch a large but unmanned rocket in a cow pasture near Magdeburg. On the first test, the rocket refused to rise at all. Two days later, it got only ten feet off the ground. After a few more mishaps, the rocket finally went up on June 29, traveled a short distance upward, and made a belly landing one thousand feet from its launching pad, getting badly damaged. It was repaired, and tested again, and failed again, and again, and again. Eventually the balky rocket disappeared into storage. There were no manned flights in Magdeburg.

The author of the *Sunday Referee*'s hoax article evidently received some of the preliminary reports of the Magdeburg fiasco. Using them as his basic material, and liberally calling on his imagination, he produced the first newspaper story of manned rocket flight—twenty-seven years too soon.

A good hoax dies hard, though. In May, 1935, a London magazine called *Pall Mall* ran an article by one W. J. Makin, called "Space Explorers." Makin told of visiting the testing grounds of the German Rocket Society and meeting that distinguished celebrity and space voyager, Herr Otto Fischer.

"Even as I shook hands with him," Makin wrote, "I realized that I was meeting the one man who had traveled through space inside a rocket and lived to tell the tale—the first passenger to enclose himself in a steel rocket of some twenty-four feet, which was shot six miles into the air. . . ."

The only thing wrong is that the meeting between Fischer and Makin could never have taken place. The testing grounds of the German Rocket Society were closed down and abandoned about five weeks after the supposed date of the Otto Fischer rocket flight. So the Makin interview could have taken place only during those five weeks. But Willy Ley was at the testing grounds at that time. He never saw or heard of a visiting Englishman named W. J. Makin. Nor, for that matter, was Otto Fischer to be found at the testing grounds late in 1933, or at any other time.

Otto Fischer's trip through space never happened. Yuri Gagarin's place in the history books is assured.

13: *The Piltdown Puzzle*

For more than forty years, the scientists who were trying to work out the pattern of man's evolution were troubled by one annoying piece of evidence that refused to make sense. According to the accepted theory, the first human beings, a million years or so ago, had been small, brutish-looking creatures with sloping foreheads, bulging browridges, and receding chins. Gradually evolution produced modern man, with his firm chin and high-vaulted skull.

220   The fossil remains that had been discovered generally

fit into this scheme. From Java, in the 1890's, had come *Pithecanthropus erectus.* A mine in Germany had yielded the jawbone of Heidelberg man. Scientists in China had found the remains of Peking man. Many other fossil skulls found in Africa and Asia contributed to the strength of the theory.

And then there was Piltdown man.

He made no sense at all. The Piltdown fossil was old; it had been found in geological strata deposited perhaps half a million years ago. Piltdown man's lower jaw was as one would expect so ancient a human fossil to be: it was underslung and apish. But the skull! It was high-vaulted, the noble skull of a man of great intelligence. It seemed almost like the skull of a modern man. The Piltdown puzzle threatened to wreck the whole theory of human evolution. If, half a million years ago, man had had a well-developed skull and an apelike jaw, all the younger human fossils no longer could be understood.

We know today, of course, the solution to the Piltdown enigma. Piltdown man was a hoax. Never had any creature with so human a skull and so primitive a jaw walked the earth. It took forty years to erase him from the human family tree, though—forty years of controversy, confusion, and doubt.

The story of Piltdown man began about 1908. An English lawyer named Charles Dawson, whose hobby was hunting for fossils, learned that workmen in a gravel pit near the village of Piltdown in Sussex had found an odd   221 skull while digging. Dawson later said that he had gone to the pit and the workmen had given him two skull fragments, stained a deep brown by the presence of iron oxide in the ground.

As Dawson told it, he conducted a systematic excavation in the gravel pit when the workmen were finished. Dawson collected nine skull fragments in all. To preserve them, he said, he bathed them in a chemical called potassium dichromate.

In the years that followed, Dawson returned to the gravel pit to find more fragments of the fossil skull. A few small pieces turned up in 1911, along with the bones of other animals, and a few flint tools. Dawson dated the age of the gravel pit as Tertiary—say, ten million years, give or take five million or so.

Realizing that he had made an important discovery, Dawson called in his friend, Arthur Smith Woodward, keeper of the department of geology at the British Museum. For more than thirty years Dawson had corresponded with the highly respected Woodward, now and then sending him fossils for evaluation.

Woodward journeyed to Sussex in 1912. He knew that if Dawson's find were genuine, it might well be the oldest fossil human relic ever discovered. Working with Dawson, Woodward succeeded in excavating another fragment of human skull. It fit exactly into the pieces Dawson had already found. But, of course, it differed in not having been stained with potassium dichromate; Wood-
222   ward had criticized Dawson for altering the color of

his earlier finds by treating them with that chemical.

Later in 1912, a new and exciting discovery appeared: an extremely primitive lower jaw, and a few teeth. The jaw was stained by iron oxide, as with all the other fossils at the site. But, mysteriously, it was also stained by potassium dichromate. Dawson had applied potassium dichromate to the skull fragments after excavating them. The jawbone, though, *already* bore the preservative stain! For reasons which we will never know, Arthur Smith Woodward did not find it at all remarkable that a fossil buried for eons should come from the earth already neatly prepared as a laboratory specimen.

Woodward took the Piltdown material to London and exhibited it in December, 1912. Speaking before the Geological Society of London, he showed his reconstruction of the fossil man. The find did not date from Tertiary times as Dawson thought, he said. In Woodward's opinion, Piltdown man had flourished in the Lower Pleistocene period, perhaps five hundred thousand years ago. The skull, which he assembled in jigsaw-puzzle fashion from the fragments, was quite human in shape, though its walls were thick and it could not have contained a very large brain. It showed none of the usual primitive features, the jutting browridges and the sloping forehead. The jawbone, on the other hand, looked like that of an ape. It was much more primitive than that of any other known human fossil.

The strange fossil quickly acquired a scientific name: *Eoanthropus dawsoni,* "Dawson's Dawn Man." The skull went on exhibit at the British Museum, proudly displayed as the first known fossil of ancient man in Britain. Woodward and Dawson returned to the now-famous gravel pit at Piltdown, and started a new excavation.

Some further skull fragments turned up, another tooth, and a wide assortment of fossil animal bones, which some scientists jokingly called the "Piltdown Zoo." The "Zoo" created some confusion of its own, for it contained, jumbled up in the same level, the bones of animals that had lived millions of years apart. There were such ancient creatures as the mastodon and the early rhinoceros, and such relatively recent ones as the beaver, red deer, and horse. What were they all doing in the same stratum?

Woodward and Dawson also found an object that looked like a cudgel, more than a foot long, rounded at one end and pointed at the other. It appeared to bear curious carvings, and Woodward described it as a weapon undoubtedly used by Piltdown man. Soon after its discovery, in 1915, two skull bones were found which Woodward declared belonged to a second specimen of Piltdown man.

Dawson, the man who had started it all, died in 1916. Arthur Smith Woodward of the British Museum became Piltdown man's "spokesman," replying to the attacks of the scientific critics. There were a great many attacks, too. The study of human evolution was less than seventy-five years old, and the existing theory had been developed only recently and with great effort. Now along came Woodward and Dawson and their Piltdown man to knock everything apart. It was easier to deny Piltdown man's existence than it was to fit him into the evolutionary scheme.

The main line of attack was that the skull and the jaw, though they had been found near one another, belonged to two separate creatures. A British anatomist named Waterston wrote that it was about as sensible to match the jaw and the skull as it was to link "a chimpanzee's foot with the bones of an essentially human thigh and leg." Many of the experts insisted that it was absurd to think there had ever been a creature with a man's skull and an ape's jaw; they called Piltdown man a monstrosity, and refused to admit him to the family tree of humanity.

Led by Woodward, Piltdown man's backers prevailed. Only a few grumbling scientists went on insisting that the jaw and skull did not go together. *Eoanthropus dawsoni* entered the textbooks, and museums throughout the world put plaster casts of the Piltdown fossil next to their casts of Pithecanthropus and other ancient men. No one could give a satisfactory explanation of Piltdown man's unusual appearance, though. All that could be said was that he must have been some kind of freak, an evolutionary offshoot in a special category of his own.

One of the dissatisfied few was Kenneth P. Oakley, a geologist affiliated with the British Museum. He had his doubts about Piltdown man, and set out in 1949 to expose him for the hoax he had to be.

Oakley had two associates in his campaign of debunking: Wilfred E. Le Gros Clark and J. S. Weiner, both of Oxford University. They obtained a few tiny slivers of bone from the Piltdown specimens and applied the fluorine test for dating.

The fluorine method had first been developed in 1844 by an English chemist named Middleton. He had found that the longer bones lie buried in the ground, the more fluorine they absorb from ground water. Since different areas have different concentrations of fluorine, the method does not give any information about the absolute age of a specimen, but it does tell which of several specimens found in the same place is older than the others.

Oakley, Weiner, and Le Gros Clark ran their fluorine tests and checked the results against the fluorine content of the tooth of a recent chimpanzee and against the fluorine content of other fossils of known antiquity from the Piltdown area. They found that the Piltdown skull's fluorine content was about the same as in fossil bones from the Upper Pleistocene, perhaps fifty thousand years old. The test showed that the Piltdown skull was definitely not Lower Pleistocene (five hundred thousand years old) as Woodward had suggested. As for the Piltdown jaw, it was quite recent, they learned. At best it had been in the ground a few decades—no more.

They studied the teeth found with the puzzling jaw. They showed heavy signs of wear; they were almost flat, in fact, and the investigators termed their flatness "much more even than that normally produced by natural wear." Under the microscope, the Piltdown teeth showed fine scratches in the enamel, as though they had been filed down deliberately to give them a more nearly human appearance. Apes, because their jaws do not work the way ours do, do not wear their molars down.

Another chemical test measured the nitrogen content of the Piltdown bones. Work done in 1947 had shown that the nitrogen content of bones preserved under the same conditions declines at a fairly constant rate. Studies carried out at the British Museum showed that the Piltdown jaw had a nitrogen content of 3.9 per cent, compared with a 4.1 per cent figure for fresh bone. The various Piltdown skull fragments, though, had nitrogen contents ranging from 0.6 per cent to 1.4 per cent as compared with the 0.7 per cent figure of an undoubtedly genuine Upper Pleistocene bone. The Piltdown teeth recorded nitrogen contents of 4.2 to 5.1 per cent, as against 3.2 per cent for a recent chimpanzee molar and 0.3 per cent for a genuine Upper Pleistocene tooth.

The nitrogen test thus confirmed the fluorine test: the Piltdown skull was reasonably ancient, possibly some fifty thousand years old, but the troublesome Piltdown jaw was not ancient at all.

There were other revealing aspects about the fossils. All the Piltdown bones had a thick reddish-brown coating, the result of iron-oxide staining while in the earth. The investigators found that the stain on the Piltdown teeth   227 was only surface-deep, and that below a coating of "a tough, flexible paint-like substance" the teeth were still white. The jawbone, too, was stained only on the surface, which indicated that it had been artificially colored to look ancient. The Piltdown skull, however, was stained through and through by the iron oxide, a sign of considerable age.

The potassium dichromate staining also came under scrutiny. It was pointed out that all the Piltdown fragments bore this staining, including the jaw. But the jaw had been found by Arthur Smith Woodward, not by Dawson—and Woodward certainly would not have applied the stain to it, since he had criticized Dawson for staining the skull fragments. The three investigators commented that the staining of the Piltdown jaw could only be explained "as a necessary part of the deliberate matching of the jaw of a modern ape with the mineralized cranial fragments."

They published their report in 1953. Its conclusion was uncompromising. "From the evidence which we have obtained, it is now clear that the distinguished paleontologists and archaeologists who took part in the excavations at Piltdown were the victims of a most elaborate and carefully prepared hoax." They remarked, though, that "the faking of the mandible and canine [the jawbone and tooth] is so extraordinarily skillful" that the hoax could not have been detected with the methods available in 1912.

228   Finally, they expressed their deeply thankful relief

that Piltdown man, with his strange mixture of human and apelike characteristics, could now be dropped from the roster of accepted human fossils.

There was a noisy outcry in the British Parliament when the exposé appeared. Indignant members of Parliament demanded to know, on November 25, 1953, how the British Museum could have been fooled by such a blatant hoax. The anthropologists who had said all along that Piltdown man had been a fraud now came forward to bow modestly and accept praise. Those who had argued in Piltdown man's favor turned away reporters with a brusque and embarrassed reply of "No comment!"

Weiner, Oakley, and Le Gros Clark followed their first studies of Piltdown man with a new report published in 1955, "Further Evidence on Piltdown." This second statement dealt with the various "tools" and "weapons" that had been found with Piltdown man. Oakley reported that the so-called cudgel was actually the bone of an elephant, carved by some recent hand to look like an ancient club. He wrote, "The ends were whittled with a steel knife, and the newly cut surfaces were stained with an iron solution." The flint tools turned out to have been shaped quite recently and given an artificial appearance of age through staining.

The fluorine-dating technique had been improved since the first Piltdown tests in 1949 and 1950, and a more precise test had shown that the Piltdown jaw and teeth had a fluorine content of less than 0.04 per cent. 229

That indicated "that whereas the skull bones were probably prehistoric, the canine tooth, the mandible, and the isolated molar were modern."

The report of Oakley, Weiner, and Le Gros Clark had fully established the fraudulent nature of Piltdown man. Someone had taken the jawbone and teeth of a modern ape—probably an orangutan, they felt—and had stained them to look ancient. The teeth had been cunningly filed down to give them a manlike appearance of wear. Then the jaw and teeth had been planted at the Piltdown site, along with the cudgel, the flint tools, and other such items. The skull, on the other hand, was probably genuine, though not nearly as old as Dawson and Woodward had thought. It was in all likelihood the fossil skull of a man who had inhabited the Piltdown region some thirty thousand to fifty thousand years ago.

That dealt adequately with Piltdown man, but a big question still remained unanswered: Who was the hoaxer?

Dawson and Woodward both were dead. No one at all suggested that Woodward could in any way have been a party to the hoax. His reputation for honesty was above suspicion. Like so many men who have become involved in famous hoaxes of science, Woodward let his enthusiasms run away with him; he wanted to believe that Piltdown man was genuine, and so he forced himself to ignore the improbable aspects of the relationship between the jaw and the skull. Woodward was a dupe, but not a hoaxer.

What about Charles Dawson?

It was hard to believe that anyone so staid and conventional as Dawson could have been responsible for such a gaudy thing as a hoax. Dawson was a stodgy, successful country lawyer. Like so many Englishmen who live in the country, Dawson dabbled a bit in scientific matters. People who had known him insisted that it was unlikely that Dawson was guilty. They suggested, instead, that some unknown friend of Dawson's had played a clever prank on him. After Dawson had found the genuine Piltdown skull, so this theory goes, the hypothetical friend had obtained an ape's jawbone, had artfully stained it and filed it to look ancient, and had planted it where Dawson was likely to find it.

This idea has some serious flaws, though. No one yet has suggested any possible friend of Dawson's who had the scientific knowledge necessary to create such a convincing-looking fake fossil, one that would keep the scientific world in turmoil for more than a generation. And was it likely that someone who had played such a clever hoax would keep quiet about it after its success? More probably, if there had been an outside hoaxer, he would have stepped forth with the real story eventually, perhaps waiting for Dawson's death before puncturing the hoax.

J. S. Weiner, who carried on an inquiry into the Piltdown hoax after the scientific part of the work was done, eliminated every figure in the story except one: Charles Dawson himself. Weiner did not, for lack of "positive   231 and final proof," name Dawson as the hoaxer, but he concluded that the evidence certainly pointed that way.

Why did he do it, if he really did?

Not for money, certainly. Dawson never made a penny from Piltdown man. But he did win fame in his own time, since the fossil was named for him—*Eoanthropus dawsoni*. Possibly this lifelong fossil-hunter deliberately cooked up Piltdown man solely to get his name into the annals of science. Or, maybe, he was troubled because no fossil of ancient man had ever been discovered in England up to his time, and so he found it necessary to invent one. (Several authentic and important human fossils have been found in England since Dawson's day.)

Dawson's motives will always remain a mystery, but J. S. Weiner did manage to turn up one clue in recent years that definitely seems to mark him as the perpetrator of the hoax.

Dawson had made his home in the town of Lewes, near Piltdown. Another resident of Lewes, one Harry Morris, had been a collector of ancient flint tools. Sometime about 1915, Morris had obtained from Dawson a flint from the Piltdown site. Soon after, Morris discovered that the flint was a fake, and jotted down a memorandum to that effect in his collection.

Morris was dead. He had left his collection to A. P. Pollard, also of Lewes, who had traded the flints to 232 Frederick Wood of nearby Ditchling for a collection of birds' eggs. Before parting with the flints, though, Pollard had noticed Morris' little note accusing Dawson of fraud. When the Piltdown hoax was exposed in 1953, Pollard realized that he had briefly been in possession of an important clue to the mystery. He got in touch with Weiner, and told him the story.

Weiner went to Ditchling to look for Frederick Wood. Wood, too, had passed away, but his wife still had the cabinet of flints that her husband had obtained from Pollard years before. There were twelve drawers of these flints in all, and the twelfth drawer contained the Piltdown flint. It was tagged with a comment in Morris' handwriting:

"Stained by C. Dawson with intent to defraud (all). —H.M."

There were two notes from Morris in the drawer also. The first repeated the charge of fraud, adding with some irritation that Dawson had given him the flint in exchange "for my most valued specimen." The second note declared that hydrochloric acid would remove the brown color that was the mark of the flint's antiquity—which Weiner found was correct. The flint tool was just a common chunk of stone, which had been chipped to look like a relic of ancient man, and then stained to conceal the recent nature of the chipping.

The Harry Morris flint is the only evidence that Charles Dawson knowingly dealt in fraudulent antiqui- 233 ties. It would not convict Dawson in a court of law, but it seems safe to name him as the most likely villain in the Piltdown story. His hunger for fame produced one of the most ingenious scientific hoaxes of all time—and kept science baffled for four decades.

A Last Word

Our gallery of rogues has become a crowded one. Cook and Koch, Dawson and Keely, Mesmer and Schliemann, and many others—they all did their bit to confuse, to deceive, and to obfuscate.

Why did they do it?

The motives are varied ones, and some emerge with cleaner hands than others. Richard Adams Locke, the author of the Moon Hoax, was simply having some journalistic fun. He meant no harm, and soon confessed. The unknown creator of the Otto Fischer rocket story did not seriously intend any major fraud, either. He, like Locke, was only a clever newspaperman at work, enlivening a dull day.

For others, profit was the motive: Fioravanti, the maker of the Etruscan statues, for example. John W. Keely, the perpetual-motion man, was an outright swindler who milked his gullible backers so that he could lead a comfortable life. Mesmer, he of animal magnetism, was a medical quack, a charlatan who could have done great harm to his patients had his career not been cut short by exposure. True, he stumbled across something of real importance—hypnotism—but that does not make him any less reprehensible. Dr. Koch, too, was of a profiteering turn of mind, though of course his manufactured sea serpents injured no one as they made him wealthy. We have seen how his biggest victim was himself, for no one would believe him when once in his life he made an important and genuine discovery.

Some of our hoaxers were out to injure the reputations of others or to win fame for themselves. The two professors who hoaxed poor Dr. Beringer were of this stripe, undoubted rascals out to ruin a harmless (if too easily duped) scholar. Perhaps Dr. Cook, too, was motivated by a desire to rob his old comrade Peary of glory, though we can never be certain what made this complex man tick.

Fame was the spur for others. In Charles Dawson and Paul Kammerer we see men so eager for scientific glory that they stooped to tampering with the evidence, thus committing the greatest sin against truth that a scientist can. Paul Schliemann, who wanted to be as famous as his grandfather, was another who sought acclaim through fraud. And possibly this is the category for the tormented and maligned Dr. Cook, who resorted to inventing accomplishments that in reality were beyond his grasp.

Then we have de Loys and his Venezuelan ape-man, possibly a hoax, possibly not. The story is too deeply shrouded in uncertainty for us to understand it or interpret motives. And lastly there is the Kensington Stone, which may be one of America's most important historical relics, or else only the work of a few amateur philologists whiling away the long Minnesota winter. Probably the real author of this hoax—if it is a hoax at all—will never be identified.

The motives are varied, but the patterns are often similar. Again and again, we see how a hoax draws in the innocent bystanders. They look at the "evidence" and are converted, and go forth to tell the world—while the hoaxer laughs into his sleeve at the ardor of these passionate disciples. Such dupes are the most pitiful victims of hoaxing: Woodward in the Piltdown case, Holand in the Kensington Stone story, and the rest. How terrible is their confusion when the hoax they back so firmly is at last unmasked!

Hoaxes have their uses, though. They provide important tests of knowledge. Piltdown man, for example, was exposed because he would not fit into a theory. The the- 237

ory looked valid, so Piltdown man had to be a fake—
and eventually he was so shown to be. If Weiner, Oakley, and Le Gros Clark had tested Piltdown man and
found him genuine, it would have brought down the theory with a resounding crash. But Piltdown man toppled
instead—and his overthrow made the theory of evolution look stronger than ever. It met and survived the
challenge of Piltdown man.

Hoaxes teach us to test, to weigh, to examine. "He that
knows nothing doubts nothing," George Herbert wrote in
1640. We do not win our knowledge cheaply. Every fact
must stand up to close scrutiny. The clever, scheming
hoaxers who for motives of mischief or profit seek to
falsify the facts of science serve in the role of devil's
advocate for knowledge. Because we know that hoaxes
are possible, we look all the more closely at what we
take to be truth. And so we learn, again and again, what
W. S. Gilbert wrote years ago: "Things are seldom what
they seem."

Bibliography

CHAPTER ONE: THE LYING STONES OF DR. BERINGER

Jahn, Melvin E., and Woolf, Daniel J. *The Lying Stones of Dr. Johann Bartholomew Adam Beringer*. Berkeley and Los Angeles: University of California Press, 1963. The first English translation of Beringer's book, plus essays on his times and on the hoax. Contains plates of the stones.

White, Andrew D. *A History of the Warfare of Science with Theology in Christendom*. New York: D. Appleton, 1896. A marvelously entertaining study of the struggle of science to free itself from the shroud of ignorance—with a section on Beringer and on the other fossil theories of his day. New ed., New York: Dover Publications, Inc., 2 vols., 1964.

CHAPTER TWO: THE MARVELOUS MAGNETISM OF DR. MESMER

Mackay, Charles. *Extraordinary Popular Delusions and the*

Madness of Crowds. London: Richard Bentley, 1841. New edition, Wells, Vermont: Fraser, 1932. A full account of Mesmer and the other magnetizers, as well as richly rewarding chapters on alchemy, the witch mania, the tulip craze, and other follies of the past.

Van Doren, Carl. *Benjamin Franklin.* New York: The Viking Press, 1938. This classic biography of Franklin tells the story of his involvement with Mesmer in Paris.

CHAPTER THREE: THE MEN ON THE MOON

Locke's Moon Hoax has been reprinted many times. The version I used appeared in a science-fiction magazine, *Amazing Stories,* September, 1926.

Ley, Willy. *Rockets, Missiles, and Space Travel.* New York: The Viking Press, 1957. A comprehensive account of space flight from its very beginnings, with some pages on the Moon Hoax.

MacDougall, Curtis D. *Hoaxes.* New York: Dover Publications, Inc., 1958. Brief, lively coverage of hundreds of hoaxes, including the Moon Hoax.

CHAPTER FOUR: THE SEA SERPENT OF DR. KOCH

Carrington, Richard. *Mermaids and Mastodons.* London: Chatto & Windus, 1957. Information about Koch's Missourium and other mastodons, and a detailed history of sea serpents.

Lucas, Frederic A. *Animals of the Past.* New York: American Museum of Natural History, 1929. Zeuglodon, mastodons, and other prehistoric creatures described.

Montagu, M. F. Ashley, and Peterson, C. Bernard. "The Earliest Account of the Association of Human Artifacts with Fossil Mammals in North America," *Proceedings of the American Philosophical Society,* Volume 87, Number 5, May 5, 1944.

Silverberg, Robert. *Home of the Red Man.* Greenwich, Conn.:

New York Graphic Society, 1963. Accounts of Figgins' Folsom discoveries and other archaeological evidence of early man in North America.

Wyman, Jeffries. "The Fossil Skeleton Recently Exhibited in New York as that of a Sea-Serpent, etc.," *Proceedings of the Boston Society of Natural History,* November, 1845.

CHAPTER FIVE: JOHN KEELY'S PERPETUAL-MOTION MACHINE

Encyclopaedia Britannica. Article, "Perpetual Motion," 14th ed.

Klein, Alexander. "Atomic Energy, 1872–1899: R.I.P." Included in *Grand Deception,* edited by Alexander Klein. Philadelphia and New York: J. B. Lippincott Company, 1955.

MacDougall, Curtis D. *Hoaxes.* New York: Dover Publications, Inc., 1958.

Schwartz, Julius. "John Worrell Keely," *Fantastic Adventures,* September, 1939.

CHAPTER SIX: THE KENSINGTON STONE

Boland, Charles Michael. *They All Discovered America.* New York: Doubleday & Company, Inc., 1961. An account of visitors to North America before Columbus, with a chapter on the Kensington Stone. The book is extremely entertaining, but Boland takes an uncritical attitude toward his material and seems willing to believe any tale of pre-Columbian visit whatever, no matter how unlikely. Naturally, he accepts the authenticity of the Kensington Stone. To be read with caution.

Herrmann, Paul. *Conquest by Man.* New York: Harper & Row, Publishers, 1954. A general history of human exploration, including a section on Viking visits to the New World. Herrmann is also pro-Kensington Stone.

Holand, Hjalmar R. *Explorations in America Before Columbus.*

241

New York: Twayne Publishers, Inc., 1956. The most recent
book by the Kensington Stone's most ardent advocate and
propagandist.

Wahlgren, Erik. *The Kensington Stone, a Mystery Solved.* Madison, Wisc.: University of Wisconsin Press, 1958. A book-length attack on the Kensington Stone, embodying the most recent scholarly findings. Wahlgren used much of the same material in his article, "The Case of the Kensington Rune Stone," *American Heritage,* April, 1959.

CHAPTER SEVEN: DR. COOK AND THE NORTH POLE

Amundsen, Roald. *My Life as an Explorer.* New York: Doubleday & Company, Inc., 1928. The conqueror of the South Pole offers some opinions, largely favorable, of Dr. Cook's character.

Berger, Meyer. *The Story of the New York Times, 1851–1951.* New York: Simon & Schuster, Inc., 1951. The journalistic background on the Cook-Peary controversy.

Bridges, E. Lucas. *Uttermost Part of the Earth.* London: Hodder & Stoughton, 1951. Adventures of the Bridges family in Tierra del Fuego, with a chapter on Dr. Cook and the Yahgan dictionary.

Cook, Frederick A. "The Discovery of the Pole." Cook's first despatch to the New York *Herald,* published on September 2, 1909, was reprinted in *National Geographic Magazine,* October, 1909.

Cook, Frederick A. *Return From the Pole.* London: Burke, 1953. Cook's last book on his alleged polar journey, not published until long after his death. This edition contains a useful essay—strongly pro-Cook—by Frederick J. Pohl, "The North Pole Controversy."

Freeman, Andrew A. *The Case for Doctor Cook.* New York:
Coward-McCann, Inc., 1961. As the title implies, a not very

objective biography with Cook as the hero and Peary in the role of the villain.

Kirwan, L. P. *The White Road*. London: Hollis & Carter, 1959. A good history of polar exploration, favorable to Peary and frowning on Cook.

Mirsky, Jeannette. *To the North*. New York: The Viking Press, 1934. Probably the best of all histories of Arctic exploration, with information on Peary and others. Miss Mirsky was sued by Cook in 1935 because she doubted that he had been to the Pole.

Weems, John Edward. *Race for the Pole*. New York: Holt, Rinehart & Winston, Inc., 1960. The Cook-Peary controversy in detail. The author regards Cook's trip as a hoax, and favors Peary's version of the race.

CHAPTER EIGHT: PAUL SCHLIEMANN AND THE LOST
CONTINENT OF ATLANTIS

Babcock, William H. *Legendary Islands of the Atlantic*. New York: American Geographical Society, 1922. Atlantis and other geographical myths.

De Camp, L. Sprague. *Lost Continents*. New York: The Gnome Press, Inc., 1954. The definitive work on the Atlantis legend. An appendix provides the text of Plato's Atlantis references.

Ley, Willy. "Schliemann's Atlantis Hoax," *Fantastic Adventures*, August, 1940.

Silverberg, Robert. *Lost Cities and Vanished Civilizations*. Philadelphia: Chilton Books, 1962. Includes a chapter on Heinrich Schliemann's work at Troy, and on the Mayan ruins of Yucatán.

Silverberg, Robert. *Empires in the Dust*. Philadelphia: Chilton Books, 1963. Discussion and illustrations of the Tiahuanaco monuments.

Bibliography

CHAPTER NINE: THE ETRUSCAN SCULPTURES

Arnau, Frank. *The Art of the Faker: 3,000 Years of Deception.* Boston: Little, Brown and Company, 1961. Although published before the exposure of the Fioravanti fraud, this book gives a good general background on art forgeries, Etruscan and otherwise.

Bloch, Raymond. *The Etruscans.* New York: Frederick A. Praeger, Inc., 1961. A well-illustrated book on Etruscan history, culture, art, and archaeology.

Parsons, Harold W. "The Art of Fake Etruscan Art," *Art News,* February, 1962. Parsons' own magazine account of the hoax exposure. See also *Time,* February 24, 1961.

Silverberg, Robert. *Empires in the Dust.* Philadelphia: Chilton Books, 1963. Includes a chapter on the Etruscan civilization.

CHAPTER TEN: THE CASE OF THE VENEZUELAN APE-MAN

Boule, Marcellin, and Vallois, Henri V. *Fossil Men.* New York: The Dryden Press, 1957. Information on the primates in general. Also a section on the theories of Fiorino Ameghino.

Wendt, Herbert. *Out of Noah's Ark.* London: Weidenfeld & Nicolson, 1959. The story of de Loys' ape-man, including the original photograph.

CHAPTER ELEVEN: THE KAMMERER TRAGEDY

Gardner, Martin. *Fads and Fallacies in the Name of Science.* New York: Dover Publications, Inc., 1957. An amusing compendium of quackery and fraud, with a valuable chapter on Lysenko, Michurin, and Lamarck.

Huxley, Julian. *Essays in Popular Science.* London: Penguin Books, 1937. Includes Huxley's review of Kammerer's 1924 book.

Ley, Willy. *Salamanders and other Wonders.* New York: The

Viking Press, 1955. The full story of the Paul Kammerer affair.

Wendt, Herbert. *In Search of Adam*. Boston: Houghton Mifflin Company, 1956. Kammerer's hoax and its relation to the theory of evolution.

CHAPTER TWELVE: OTTO FISCHER'S ROCKET RIDE

Ley, Willy. "Fantastic Hoaxes," *Fantastic Adventures*, January, 1940. Short account of Ley's exposure of the Otto Fischer hoax.

Ley, Willy. *Rockets, Missiles, and Space Travel*. New York: The Viking Press, 1957. The story of the German Rocket Society and of early rocket research.

Wonder Stories, March, 1934. Reprint of a condensed version of the original hoax news story.

CHAPTER THIRTEEN: THE PILTDOWN PUZZLE

Boule, Marcellin, and Vallois, Henri V. *Fossil Men*. New York: The Dryden Press, 1957. The scientific data on the Piltdown story.

Heizer, Robert F. (ed.). *Man's Discovery of His Past*. Englewood Cliffs, N.J.: Prentice-Hall, Inc., 1962. This anthology includes both the 1953 and 1955 scientific reports on Piltdown man by Oakley, Weiner, and Le Gros Clark.

Weiner, J. S. *The Piltdown Forgery*. New York: Oxford University Press, 1955. The full story of the exposure of the hoax.

Index

247

Index

248

University of Nebraska Press

Also of Interest:

THE COMING OF THE FAIRIES
By Sir Arthur Conan Doyle
Introduction by John M. Lynch

Sir Arthur Conan Doyle (1859–1930), best known as the author of Sherlock
Holmes stories but also a devout spiritualist, was entirely convinced by a
set of photographs apparently showing two young girls from Cottingley
in Yorkshire playing with a group of tiny, translucent fairies. Originally
published in 1922, Doyle's book lays out the story of the photographs, their
supposed provenance, and the implications of their existence. This quirky
and fascinating book allows us to get inside the mind of an intelligent,
highly respected man who happened to believe in fairies.

ISBN 0-8032-6655-3; 978-0-8032-6655-1

INVENTED EDEN
The Elusive, Disputed History of the Tasaday
By Robin Hemley

In 1971 Manual Elizalde, a Philippine government minister with a dubious
background, discovered a band of twenty-six "Stone Age" rain-forest
dwellers living in total isolation. The tribe was soon featured in American
newscasts and graced the cover of *National Geographic*. But after a series
of aborted anthropological ventures, the Tasaday Reserve established
by Ferdinand Marcos was closed to visitors, and the tribe vanished
from public view. Twelve years later, a Swiss reporter hiked into the area
and discovered that the Tasaday were actually farmers whom Elizalde
had coerced into dressing in leaves and posing with stone tools. The
"anthropological find of the century" had become the "ethnographic hoax
of the century." Or maybe not. Robin Hemley tells a story that is more
complex than either the hoax proponents or the authenticity advocates
might care to admit. It is a gripping and ultimately tragic tale of innocence
found, lost, and found again.

ISBN 0-8032-7363-0; 978-0-8032-7363-4